Better Homes and Gardens

VEGETABLE COOK BOOK

MEREDITH PRESS
New York Des Moines

Printed in the United States of America.
Third Printing, 1968.

contents

This checked seal tells you that every recipe in your Vegetable Cook Book is endorsed by the Better Homes and Gardens Test Kitchen. Each recipe is tested over and over till it rates high in family appeal, practicality, and downright deliciousness!

Better Homes and Gardens TEST KITCHEN

vegetables

Vegetables belong to the good things of life. Vegetables provide many of the finest flavors we know. To get those flavors, treat them with care, the same as with those other good things.

Thanks to science, everyone is now aware that we eat vegetables to keep healthy. Vegetarians said they were good long before science had much notion why. Until lately cooks weren't enterprising about accepting ways to make them as cheerful to the soul as beneficial to the body.

This is the book for those who would cook vegetables for the joy of eating them, for those who like to try a new vegetable or a new method for preparing an old one. In our so-big country, climate and soil are so varied that we produce almost every vegetable known, and throughout the year, bridging the seasons with their variety.

Anyone with a will can learn to recognize the best qualities in a vegetable, from an artichoke to a zucchini. Our many-times-tested recipes are intended to beguile you into experimenting with new combinations, flavorings, sauces. We assure hearty enjoyment of the finished product. For our pictures we chose vegetable specimens less than a day out of the fields to emphasize the endless variety in their shape and color, hoping to have in you a new champion for vegetables.

BASIC COOKING GUIDE

Vegetable	How to prepare	How to cook	Time
Artichokes French or globe	Wash. Cut off 1 inch of top, the stem, and tips of leaves. Pull off any loose leaves. Brush cut edges with lemon juice.	Place in large amount boiling salted water. (Add ¼ cup olive oil and few cloves garlic, or lemon slices.) Cover; simmer till leaf pulls out easily. Drain.	25-30 min.
Jerusalem	Wash, pare; leave whole or slice.	Cook covered in small amount boiling salted water.	15-35 min.
Asparagus	Wash; scrub gently with vegetable brush. If sandy, scrape off the scales. Break stalks—they will snap where tender part starts.	Cut up; cook covered in a small amount of boiling salted water. Or cook whole spears covered in small amount boiling salted water.	8-10 min. 10-15 min.
Beans Green or wax	Wash; remove ends and strings. Cook whole or in 1-inch pieces. Or slit lengthwise.	Cook covered in a small amount of boiling salted water.	20-30 min. 10-12 min.
Lima, fresh	Shell and wash.	Cook covered in small amount boiling salted water.	20-30 min.
Lima, dried	Rinse; add to 2½ times as much water as beans. Soak overnight. Or, bring to boil; simmer 2 minutes; let stand at least 1 hour.	Add salt, cover, and simmer in water used for soaking.	1 hour
Navy, dried	Prepare same as dried Limas, but use 3 times as much water as beans.	Cook same as dried Limas.	1½ hours
Beets	Cut off all but 1 inch of stems and root. Wash and scrub thoroughly. Do not pare.	Cook covered in boiling salted water. Peel when done.	35-60 min.
	Or pare and slice or cube. Or pare and shred.	Cook covered in small amount boiling salted water.	15-20 min. 10 min.
Beet greens	Wash thoroughly. Don't cut off tiny beets.	Salt lightly; cook covered without water except drops that cling to leaves. Reduce heat when steam forms. Turn with fork frequently.	5-15 min.
Broccoli	Remove outer leaves and tough part of stalks. Split rest of stalk almost to flowerets.	Tie stalks in bundle, using folded strip of foil. Stand up in 1 inch boiling salted water. Cover and cook.	15-20 min.
	Or cut in 1-inch pieces.	Cook stalk pieces covered in boiling salted water to cover 5 to 8 minutes; add flowerets.	10-15 min. total
Brussels sprouts	Cut off wilted leaves. Wash. Leave whole.	Cook covered in small amount boiling salted water.	10-15 min.
Cabbage (Green)	Remove wilted outer leaves. Cut in 6 to 8 wedges. Or shred.	Cook covered in small amount boiling salted water. Or cook wedges uncovered in cooking liquid from corned beef or ham.	10-12 min. 5-7 min. 12-15 min.

Vegetable	How to prepare	How to cook	Time
Carrots	Wash and pare or scrape. Leave whole, slice, or cut in quarters or strips.	Cook covered in a small amount of boiling, salted water.	Whole, 20-25 min. Cut up, 15-20 min.
Cauliflower	Remove leaves and some of the woody stem. Leave whole or separate into flowerets.	Cook covered in a small amount of boiling, salted water.	Whole, 20-25 min. Flowerets, 10-15 min.
Celeriac (celery root)	Cut off leaves and root fibers. Scrape or pare; dice.	Cook covered in a small amount of boiling, salted water.	20-25 min.
Celery	Cut off leaves; trim roots. Scrub thoroughly. Slice outer branches; cut hearts lengthwise.	Cook covered in a small amount of boiling, salted water, or in consomme.	10-15 min.
Chard, Swiss	Wash thoroughly; if not young, cut midribs from leaves.	Cook covered in very small amount boiling, salted water. If not young, cook midribs 10-15 minutes; then add leaves.	10-20 min. 15-25 min. total
Corn	Remove husks from fresh corn. Remove silks with stiff brush. Rinse. Cook whole. Or, cut off just tips from kernels with sharp knife and scrape cobs with dull edge of knife.	Cook covered in a small amount of boiling, salted water or uncovered in boiling, salted water to cover. Cook covered in a small amount of boiling, salted water or in milk or butter.	6-8 min. 5-8 min.
Dandelion greens	Discard greens with blossom or bud as they will be bitter. Cut off roots; wash thoroughly.	Cook covered in very small amount boiling, salted water. Turn with fork frequently.	10-20 min.
Eggplant	Wash; pare if skin is tough. Cut in ½-inch slices.	Dip in beaten egg, then in fine dry bread crumbs or corn-flake crumbs. Brown slowly on both sides in hot fat. Season.	About 4 min. total
Kohlrabi	Cut off leaves; wash, pare, and dice or slice.	Cook covered in a small amount of boiling, salted water.	25-30 min.
Leeks	Cut off green tops to within 2 inches of white part. Wash.	Cook covered in a small smount of boiling, salted water.	15-20 min.
Lentils, dried	Wash. Add to 2½ times as much water.	Cook covered at simmering till tender.	About 35 min.
Mushrooms	Wash. Cut off tips of stems. Leave whole or slice.	Add to melted butter in skillet; sprinkle with flour; mix. Cover and cook over low heat. Turn occasionally.	8-10 min.
Okra	Wash pods. Cut off stems. Cut large pods in ½-inch slices.	Cook covered in a small amount of boiling, salted water.	8-15 min.

Vegetable	How to prepare	How to cook	Time
Onions	Peel under water. Quarter, or leave small onions whole.	Cook covered in a small amount of boiling, salted water.	25-35 min.
Parsnips	Wash; pare or scrape. Slice crosswise or lengthwise.	Cook covered in a small amount of boiling, salted water.	15-20 min.
Peas Green	Shell and wash.	Cook covered in a small amount of boiling, salted water.	8-15 min.
Black-eyed	Prepare same as dried Limas.	Cook same as dried Limas.	35-45 min.
Potatoes Irish	Scrub thoroughly. Cook with skins on. Or wash and pare thinly. Cook whole, quarter, or cube.	Whole—Cook covered in boiling, salted water to cover; drain. Cut up—Cook tightly covered in small amount of boiling, salted water; drain immediately.	Whole, 25-40 min. Quartered, 20-25 min. Cubed, 10-15 min.
New	Scrub; pare narrow strip of peel from center of each. Or scrape.	Cook in boiling, salted water. Drain. Peel if desired.	Tiny 15-20 min.
Sweet	Scrub; cut off woody portions. Cook while in jackets.	Cook covered in boiling, salted water to cover. Drain at once. Peel if desired.	30-40 min.
Rutabagas	Wash, pare thinly. Slice or cube.	Cook covered in a small amount of boiling, salted water. Mash if desired.	25-40 min.
Salsify (oyster plant)	Wash; pare thinly. Slice or cube.	Cook covered in a small amount of boiling, salted water.	15-20 min.
Spinach	Cut off roots; wash several times in lukewarm water, lifting out of water each time.	Cook covered without water except drops that cling to leaves. Reduce heat when steam forms. Turn with fork frequently.	3-5 min.
Squash Acorn	Wash. Cut in half; remove seeds.	Bake cut side down at 350° 35 to 40 min.; turn cut side up; bake till done.	50-60 min.
	Or pare and cube.	Cook cubed squash covered in small amount boiling, salted water.	About 15 min.
Hubbard	Wash; cut in serving pieces; do not pare.	Place on baking sheet; season and dot with butter. Cover with foil. Bake at 350°.	1¼ hours
	Or pare and cube.	Cook covered in small amount of boiling, salted water.	About 15 min.
Summer	Wash; pare. Slice or cube.	Cook covered in a small amount of boiling, salted water.	15-20 min.
Zucchini (Italian)	Wash; do not pare. Slice thin.	Season and cook covered in butter in skillet 5 minutes; uncover and cook, turning slices, till tender.	About 10 min. total
Tomatoes	Wash ripe tomatoes. Plunge in boiling water, then cool under cold water. Peel; cut out stems. Cut up. (Or cook whole.)	Cook slowly, covered without adding water. Season with salt, pepper, and sugar. Add a little minced onion.	10-15 min.
Turnips	Wash; pare thinly. Slice or cube.	Cook covered in a small amount of boiling, salted water. Mash if desired.	15-20 min.

NUTRITION SUMMARY

	vitamin A (carotenoids)	thiamine (vitamin B1)	riboflavin (vitamin B2)	niacin (nicotinic acid)	vitamin C (ascorbic acid)	iron (Fe)
artichoke				fair		good
asparagus	good	good	good	good	good	fair
green beans	fair		fair		fair	
lima beans		excellent	fair	fair	good	excellent
broccoli	excellent	fair	excellent		excellent	fair
brussels sprouts	fair	fair	good		good	good
cabbage					good	
carrots	excellent					
cauliflower		fair	fair		excellent	fair
corn	fair	good	good	good		
mushrooms		fair	excellent	excellent		
peas	fair	excellent	fair		fair	fair
peppers	fair				excellent	
white potatoes		fair		good	good	
sweet potatoes	excellent	fair			good	
spinach	excellent	fair	excellent		excellent	excellent
winter squash	excellent		fair			
summer squash	fair			fair	good	
tomatoes	good				good	
turnips					good	

key				
	🌰 🌰 🌰	excellent source		
	🌰 🌰	good source		
	🌰	fair source		

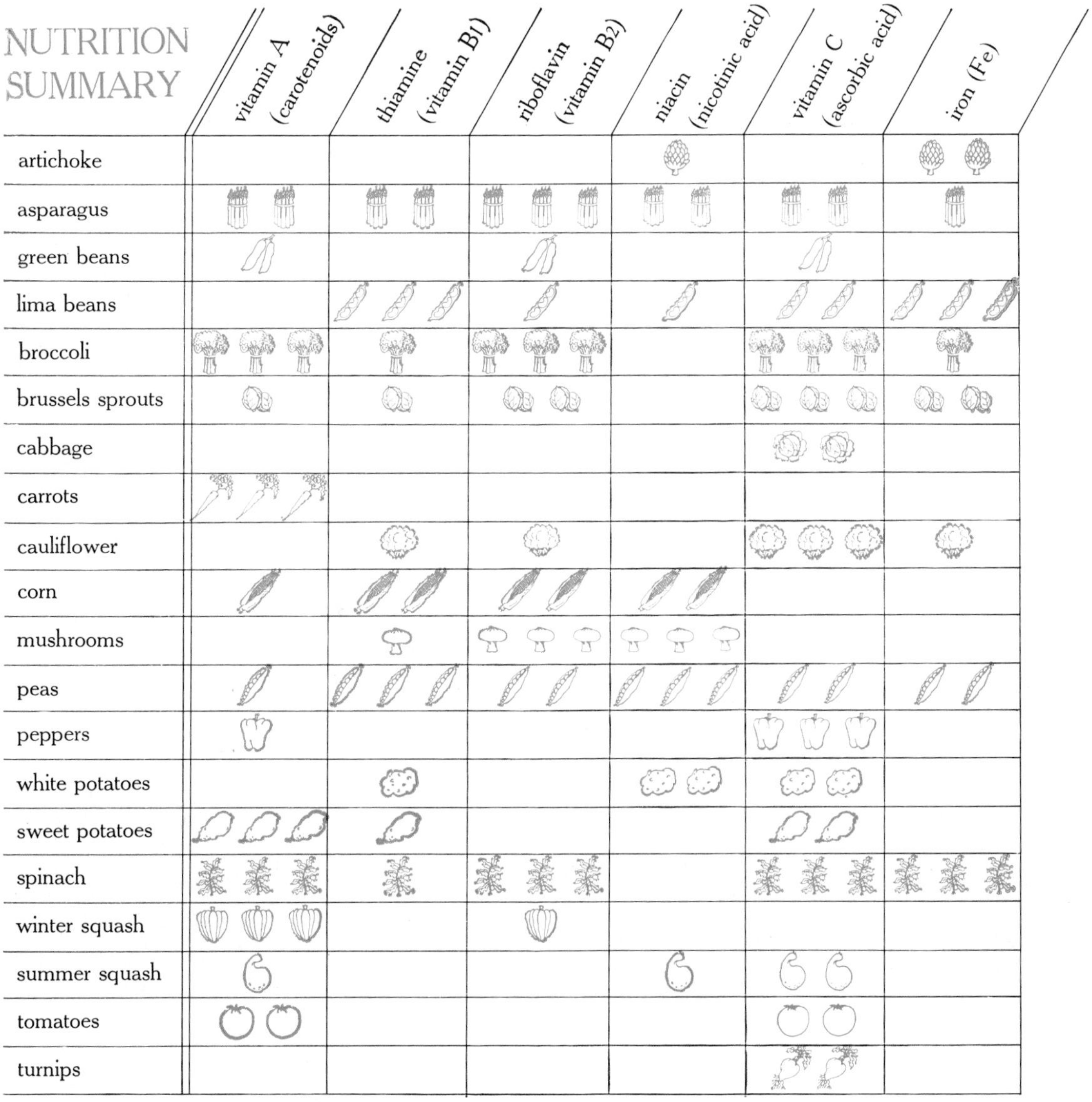

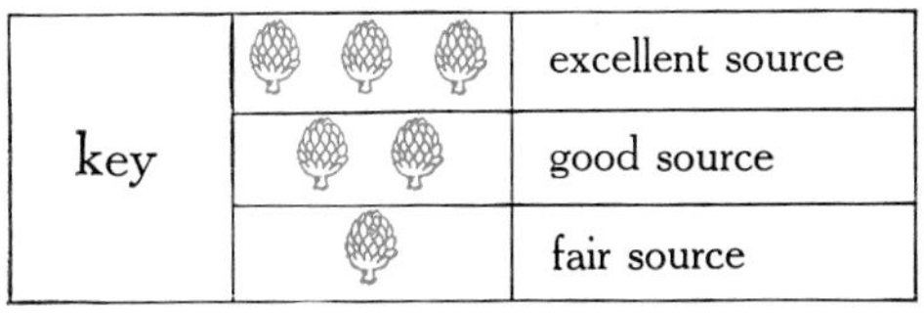

Source: *The Composition of Foods*, U.S. Department of Agriculture, 1963. The nutrient contribution of 100 grams raw edible portion was compared to that of other food sources.

Vegetables abound in vitamins and minerals. Let's see what special contributions these nutrients make to good health.

Vitamin A is needed for healthy skin, normal eyesight, and germ-resistant linings of the nose, throat, and lungs.

Thiamine helps insure normal digestion and normal functioning of nervous tissue.

Riboflavin and *niacin* play important roles in the metabolic processes of the body.

Vitamin C helps keep connecting material between the cells in good condition to prevent bleeding gums and easily bruised flesh.

Iron, a mineral element, is found in the hemoglobin of the blood which carries oxygen to all the cells of the body.

artichokes

It's unlikely that you'd ever voluntarily eat a thistle, but if you've ever eaten a globe artichoke, that's what you've done. Look above at its fascinating structure. The "heart" is actually a tiny, whole artichoke. The casing and round trimmed bottom are both parts of the whole artichoke. To eat a cooked whole artichoke, pull off the thick-based leaves dipping the stem end in melted butter or a tart sauce. Then draw off the flesh between the teeth and discard the rest of the spiny leaf. This is, to many, the greatest fascination of this aristocratic vegetable. After all the leaves have been removed, the fuzzy center or "choke" can be seen. With knife and fork, cut out and discard the choke (it's prickly if eaten). Left then for complete enjoyment is the bottom. It is important when shopping for artichokes to select heavy tight heads. Pass over any that have opened or curled leaves. To store, place the whole artichoke unwashed in a plastic bag and refrigerate. They'll keep this way for two to three weeks.

To clean fresh artichokes, give them a shower of cold running water. With sharp knife, cut off about 1 inch from top. Chop stem close to base. Pull off loose leaves around bottom. Snip sharp leaf tips off with scissors. Brush cut edges with lemon juice to keep from getting brown.

To cook bottoms, break off stem and lower leaves. Trim base with sharp knife. Cut top leaves ½ inch above base. Scoop out choke; shape into cup. Rub with lemon juice. Cook in boiling water with small amount vinegar till tender.

To cook whole artichokes, add one tablespoon salad oil to a large pan of salted water. Bring to boiling; add 5 to 6 prepared fresh artichokes (a few lemon slices may be added). Cover; simmer 20 to 30 minutes till stem is tender and a leaf pulls easily from the base. Serve hot or cold with tart dipping sauce.

ARTICHOKE VELVET

2 9-ounce packages frozen artichoke hearts
1 pint fresh mushrooms, sliced
2 tablespoons butter or margarine
One 1 1/16-ounce package chicken gravy mix
1 cup water
Dash *each* thyme and marjoram
4 ounces Swiss cheese, diced (1 cup)
1 tablespoon dry white wine

Cook artichokes according to package directions; drain. Cook mushrooms in butter till tender. Combine artichokes and mushrooms in 1-quart casserole. Prepare chicken gravy mix using package directions. Remove from heat; add herbs and cheese; stir till cheese melts. Add wine; pour over vegetables. Bake covered at 350° for 30 minutes. Serves 6 to 8.

ARTICHOKES IN CHEESE SAUCE

An elegant hurry-up entree for surprise guests. Great with a tart fruit salad—

1 9-ounce package frozen artichoke hearts
1 11-ounce can condensed Cheddar cheese soup
1 7¾-ounce can (1¾ cups) crab, drained and flaked
Freshly ground pepper
Cooked rice

Cook artichoke hearts according to package directions; drain. Combine cheese soup and flaked crab. Add artichoke hearts; cook over medium heat until heated through. Top mixture with freshly ground pepper. Serve on a bed of cooked rice. Makes 6 servings.

FILLED ARTICHOKES

4 or 5 whole fresh artichokes
¼ cup butter or margarine, melted
3 tablespoons all-purpose flour
1 cup light cream
1 cup chicken broth
1 teaspoon salt
½ teaspoon tarragon
2 cups diced cooked chicken
2 tablespoons sherry

With a sharp knife, cut off stems of artichokes. Slice off top third of each. Using a melon-ball cutter or a sharp-edged spoon, thoroughly scoop out fuzzy choke and enough additional center leaves to make a generous hollow. Remove all coarse outer leaves. Set casings upright in small amount boiling salted water. Cover and simmer for 25 to 30 minutes or till you can pierce stalk easily with fork or pull out a leaf readily. Remove and turn upside down to drain.

In a saucepan, blend butter and flour; stir in cream and broth. Cook over medium heat, stirring constantly, till sauce thickens and bubbles. Mix in salt, tarragon, and chicken. Heat through. Just before serving, stir in sherry. Spoon into the hot cooked casings. Makes 4 or 5 servings.

ARTICHOKES AND CRAB

Cut off stems of 3 or 4 artichokes; dip bases in lemon juice to prevent turning dark. Remove all leaves and fuzzy chokes. Trim bottoms to make smooth—cut around outside edge with a sweeping circular motion (as if peeling an apple) till light-colored meat is visible. Rub with lemon juice and small amount vinegar. Cook bottoms, covered, in small amount boiling salted water till just tender. Chill well.

Make a sauce combining 1 tablespoon warm water, ¾ teaspoon tarragon, crumbled, and ½ teaspoon chervil. Let stand 10 minutes. Blend herbs with 1 cup mayonnaise, 1 tablespoon drained mashed capers, 2 teaspoons Dijon-style mustard, and ½ teaspoon anchovy paste. Chill well.

Place tomato slices in crisp lettuce cups; top each with a chilled artichoke bottom*, then about ¼ cup flaked crab meat. Spoon sauce over; garnish with capers.

*Or use chilled canned artichoke bottoms.

ARTICHOKES WITH CRAB STUFFING

Leafy cups hold a luscious hot salad—

2 6½-ounce cans (2 cups) crab meat, drained
1 cup cubed process Swiss cheese
⅓ cup chopped green pepper
¼ cup finely chopped onion
1 teaspoon salt

• • •

½ cup mayonnaise or salad dressing
2 teaspoons lemon juice
5 cooked medium artichokes

Break crab meat in chunks; toss with cheese, green pepper, onion, and salt. Blend mayonnaise and lemon juice; add to crab mixture and toss lightly. Remove small center leaves of each artichoke, leaving a cup. Carefully remove choke. Fill artichokes with crab salad; place in large casserole or baking dish. Pour hot water around artichokes to depth of 1 inch. Cover and bake in moderate oven (375°) about 35 minutes or until heated through. Makes 5 servings.

MARINATED ARTICHOKES

Artichokes take on the good tang of the marinade; no other sauce needed—

4 cups water
1 cup vinegar
¼ cup olive or salad oil
4 cloves garlic, cut in half

• • •

5 to 8 artichokes

• • •

½ cup salad oil
⅓ cup wine vinegar
2 tablespoons chopped parsley
1 clove garlic, minced

Combine water, 1 cup vinegar, ¼ cup oil, and 4 cloves garlic; bring to boiling. Add artichokes and cook uncovered 25 to 30 minutes or till you can pull leaf out easily. Lift artichokes from water; drain upside down. Cut in half and trim, removing choke. Place in shallow baking dish; add salad oil, wine vinegar, parsley, and minced garlic. Let stand in refrigerator overnight; spoon marinade over once or twice. Serves 5 to 8.

asparagus

Confucius might have said: "Better to skip vegetable entirely than to overcook it!" Pictured above, Oriental Asparagus proves the merit of this counsel on vegetable cookery. The slender bias-cut stalks of this vegetable couldn't taste better!

Spring is here when fresh asparagus appears on the produce counter. Raw or cooked, hot or cold, this tender green vegetable remains a delicacy. It's been used in salads and appetizers, souffles and soups, and certainly sauced a million different ways. An interesting fact of its growth is that while asparagus plants take three years to establish themselves, they may remain productive for as long as 30 to 35 years. You can almost see asparagus growing. When the tiny spears start to appear above the ground, they may shoot up 8 to 10 inches in one day.

To choose the best quality in asparagus, look for straight stalks that are green and tender (though not rubbery) the full length. The tiny buds at the top of each stalk should be dark green or bluish green and closed tightly. The longer they've been cut, the more these buds will spread. Snapping the stalk, not cutting, will tell you where the woody part stops and the tender area begins.

ASPARAGUS-CHEESE BAKE

2 10-ounce packages frozen cut asparagus
1 8-ounce can (½ cup) small white onions, drained
4 slices bacon
1 tablespoon all-purpose flour
½ cup tomato juice
1 cup shredded sharp process cheese
1 tablespoon prepared mustard

Cook and drain asparagus, reserving ¼ cup liquid. Arrange asparagus and onions in 10x6x1½-inch baking dish. Fry bacon; drain, reserving 1 tablespoon fat. Blend flour into fat; add tomato juice and asparagus liquid. Cook and stir till thick. Add cheese and mustard; stir till smooth. Pour over vegetables; stir lightly. Crumble bacon over top. Bake at 375° for 20 minutes. Serves 6.

ASPARAGUS STICKS

Cook one 10-ounce package frozen asparagus spears using package directions; drain. Combine 2 tablespoons water, ¼ teaspoon celery salt, dash pepper, and 1 beaten egg. Roll asparagus in ½ cup fine dry bread crumbs; dip in egg mixture and roll in crumbs. Brown in 3 tablespoons butter about 5 to 8 minutes; turn occasionally. Serves 4.

ASPARAGUS IN BLANKETS

1 10-ounce package frozen asparagus spears
2 cups packaged biscuit mix
2 tablespoons butter, melted
1 2½-ounce jar dried beef

Cook asparagus in boiling salted water according to package directions. Prepare biscuit mix according to package directions for rolled biscuits. Divide dough in half; roll in two 12-inch circles. Brush with butter. Cut each circle into 6 wedges. Divide asparagus and dried beef into 12 equal portions and place crosswise on wide end of wedges; roll. Bake on greased baking sheet at 450° for 10 minutes or till done. Serve with *Cheese Sauce:* Mix one 11-ounce can Cheddar cheese soup and ¼ teaspoon crushed marjoram; heat through. Makes 6 servings.

CREAMY ASPARAGUS

Clean 2 pounds fresh asparagus and cut in 1½-inch lengths. Cook asparagus in boiling, salted water for 10 minutes; drain well. In a saucepan, combine one 10½-ounce can condensed cream of mushroom soup, ½ cup light cream, 1 teaspoon lemon juice, and 1 beaten egg; season to taste with salt and pepper. Heat thoroughly.

Pour mushroom sauce over drained asparagus; stir in ½ cup slivered blanched almonds, toasted. Serve in 5 or 6 patty shells or over toast points. Makes 5 or 6 servings.

ASPARAGUS CASSEROLE

2 tablespoons butter or margarine
2 tablespoons all-purpose flour
2 cups milk
½ teaspoon salt
Dash pepper
2 pounds fresh asparagus, cut crosswise in 1½-inch pieces (4 cups) and cooked
4 hard-cooked eggs, sliced
¼ cup (6) medium cracker crumbs
2 tablespoons butter *or* margarine, melted

Melt butter; blend in flour. Add milk all at once; cook, stirring constantly till mixture comes to a boil and thickens. Add salt and pepper. Arrange ½ of the cooked asparagus and all the egg slices in the bottom of an 8x8x2-inch baking dish. Add ½ the white sauce. Top with remaining cooked asparagus and sauce. Toss crumbs with butter; sprinkle atop sauce. Bake in a moderate oven (350°) for 30 to 35 minutes, or till heated through. Makes 6 servings.

ASPARAGUS WITH ALMOND BUTTER SAUCE

Cook 2 pounds fresh asparagus spears *or* two 10-ounce packages frozen asparagus spears in boiling salted water till tender; drain well. Cook ¼ cup slivered almonds in ¼ cup butter over low heat till golden brown, about 5 to 7 minutes, stirring constantly. Remove from heat; add ½ teaspoon salt and 1 tablespoon lemon juice and pour over asparagus. Makes 6 servings.

To prepare fresh spears for Asparagus Oriental, snap off and discard woody base of stalks. Slice asparagus with long slanting cuts (almost as you would in Frenching green beans). Keep the pieces thin—about ¼-inch thick.

To cook fresh asparagus in an asparagus cooker, lay cleaned asparagus spears on the perforated rack. Lower it into boiling salted water—just enough to barely cover asparagus. Cook stalks covered till just tender, 10 to 15 minutes. To drain, lift rack from cooker.

Make your own cooker. Fold a strip of aluminum foil to place across bottom and sides of pan, extending over edges.

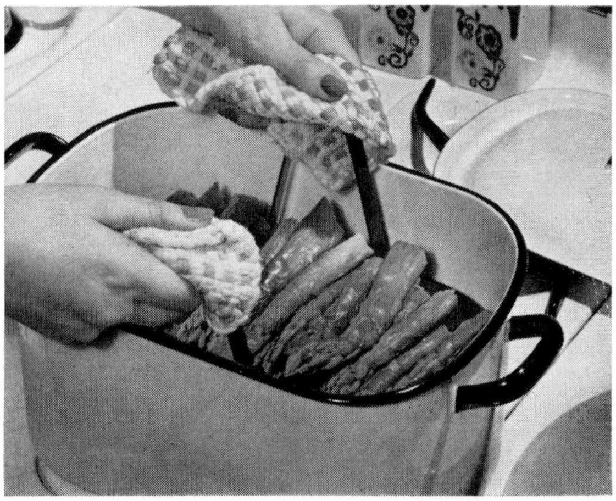

WAYS TO COOK FRESH ASPARAGUS

In skillet: Lay fresh asparagus spears flat in a skillet. Cook covered in small amount of boiling salted water just till tender, 10 to 15 minutes. To avoid overcooking the tender tips, prop them up out of water with crushed aluminum foil at one side of the pan—tips will cook in steam while the stalks cook in boiling water.

Standing up: Fasten fresh asparagus spears in a bundle—easy with a band of folded aluminum foil. Stand stalks upright in boiling salted water in a deep kettle or glass percolator. (If they fall over, prop them up again with crumpled aluminum foil.) Let tips extend 1 inch above water. Cover. Tips cook in the steam, while stalks cook in boiling water—takes 10 to 15 minutes.

ASPARAGUS ORIENTAL

Serve it still a little crunchy. The quick-cooking trick is in the cutting—

1 tablespoon salad oil
3 cups fresh asparagus in bias-cut pieces, 1½ inches long
½ teaspoon salt
½ teaspoon monosodium glutamate
Dash pepper

Heat large skillet; add salad oil, and when hot, add the asparagus. Sprinkle with seasonings. Cover. Lift skillet slightly above *high* heat and shake it constantly while cooking. Cook asparagus only till tender, 4 to 5 minutes. Reduce heat to medium if necessary, during last minute or so of cooking. Don't overcook! Makes 6 servings.

beans

Through the years, the favorite bedtime story of *Jack and the Beanstalk* has made bean fans out of sleepy tads. Perhaps this early influence partially explains the grand popularity of beans.

The many hues and shapes of common bean varieties provide a field day for photographers. Shapely jars are filled with shell beans—the brown speckled pinto beans, white navy beans, red kidney beans, green Limas, and black beans. Even the bean plants make picture-pretty gardens. Some climbing beans decorate flower beds with bright red and purple blooms.

The familiar green snap and yellow wax beans are actually immature bean pods. A quick test for freshness—bend the pod in half between your fingers; it should be crisp enough to snap easily. Bulging pods mark the tough, more mature beans which are poor quality.

Light green or white Limas are dubbed "sugar beans" for their predominant sweet flavor. Although the shelled form is pictured, fresh pods are available in many markets. When buying fresh Limas, choose dark green, well-filled pods.

Italian or fava beans, pictured in foreground, are relative newcomers to America. The long velvety pods, well known to epicures, resemble those of the Limas and have similar quality characteristics. These, as all fresh beans, should be refrigerated in plastic bags until ready for use.

SPEEDY BROWN BEANS

1 1-pound can (2 cups) dark red kidney beans
1 tablespoon brown sugar
2 teaspoons cornstarch
¼ teaspoon cinnamon
1 tablespoon vinegar

Drain kidney beans, *reserving liquid.* In saucepan combine brown sugar, cornstarch, and cinnamon. Stir in vinegar and bean liquid. Cook and stir over medium heat till mixture thickens and boils. Add drained beans; simmer over low heat for 20 minutes, stirring occasionally. Makes 3 or 4 servings.

KIDNEY-BEAN CASSEROLE

2 1-pound cans (4 cups) dark red kidney beans
8 slices bacon
½ cup chopped onion
⅓ cup chili sauce
Salt and pepper

Drain beans, *reserving 3 tablespoons liquid.* Cook bacon till crisp; drain, *reserving 2 tablespoons drippings.* Crumble bacon.

Cook onion in reserved bacon drippings till tender but not brown. Add beans, reserved 3 tablespoons bean liquid, bacon, chili sauce, salt and pepper. Pour into ungreased 1-quart casserole. Cover and bake in moderate oven (350°) for 20 minutes or till heated through. Makes 4 to 6 servings.

MAPLE BAKED BEANS

6 slices bacon

• • •

½ cup catsup
½ cup maple-flavored syrup
1 tablespoon prepared mustard
1 tablespoon instant minced onion
2 1-pound cans (4 cups) pork and beans in tomato sauce
½ cup chopped celery

Cook bacon till crisp; crumble. Combine bacon and *2 tablespoons* drippings with remaining ingredients. Pour into 10x6x1½-inch baking dish. Bake in moderate oven (350°) for 1¼ hours. Makes 4 to 6 servings.

HASH 'N BAKED BEANS

2 1-pound cans (4 cups) pork and beans in tomato sauce
1 tablespoon instant minced onion
2 teaspoons prepared horseradish
1 tablespoon prepared mustard
1 15-ounce can corned beef hash, chilled
1 8½-ounce can pineapple slices, drained
2 tablespoons brown sugar

Combine beans, onion, horseradish, and mustard in 8x8x2-inch baking dish. Cut chilled corned beef hash in 8 slices; arrange with pineapple slices atop beans. Sprinkle brown sugar over all. Bake in hot oven (400°) for 30 to 35 minutes. Serves 4 to 6.

GINGER BEAN BAKE

2 1-pound cans (4 cups) pork and beans in tomato sauce
½ cup fine gingersnap crumbs
¼ cup catsup
2 tablespoons light molasses
½ teaspoon salt

• • •

1 12-ounce can luncheon meat, sliced

Combine all ingredients except luncheon meat. Turn into 1-quart casserole. Place luncheon meat slices atop. Cover and bake in moderate oven (350°) for 30 minutes till heated through. Makes 4 to 6 servings.

APPLE-BEAN BAKE

2 1-pound cans (4 cups) pork and beans in tomato sauce
¼ cup light molasses
2 tablespoons cider vinegar
2 tablespoons prepared mustard
1 1-pound 4-ounce can (2½ cups) unsweetened sliced apples, drained

Turn beans into 1½-quart casserole. Combine molasses, vinegar, and mustard; blend into beans. Gently stir *half* the apples into bean mixture. Arrange remaining apple slices on top. Cover and bake in moderate oven (350°) for 1½ hours. Uncover and bake 30 minutes longer. Makes 6 to 8 servings.

SAUCY BAKED BEANS

So good, folks won't believe you didn't start these beans from scratch!—

6 slices bacon, cut in 1-inch pieces
3 1-pound cans (6 cups) baked beans in pork and molasses sauce
1 8-ounce can (1 cup) tomato sauce
1 cup chopped onion
½ cup catsup
¼ cup brown sugar
2 tablespoons prepared mustard
1 teaspoon salt
4 drops bottled hot pepper sauce

Cook bacon till almost crisp; drain. Mix together beans, bacon, and remaining ingredients. Bake, uncovered, in 2-quart casserole or bean pot in slow oven (300°) for 3 to 5 hours. Makes 6 servings.

PEACHY GINGER BEANS

2 1-pound cans (4 cups) pork and beans in tomato sauce
½ cup dark corn syrup
1 teaspoon instant minced onion
½ to 1 teaspoon ginger
1 pound (8 to 10) frankfurters
. . .
1 1-pound can (2 cups) peach halves, drained
Orange marmalade

Pour beans into 11½x7½x1½-inch baking dish. Combine syrup, onion, and ginger; stir into beans. Place frankfurters in bean mixture. Bake in slow oven (325°) for 45 minutes. Top with peach halves, cut side up. Fill each peach cavity with 1 teaspoon orange marmalade. Return to oven and bake 45 minutes. Makes 6 to 8 servings.

QUICK BEAN SKILLET

In skillet, melt 2 tablespoons butter or margarine. Add 1 cup diced tomato, ½ teaspoon crushed oregano, and ¼ teaspoon garlic powder. Cook a minute or so to blend flavors. Add two 1-pound cans (4 cups) beans and franks in tomato sauce.

Heat, stirring often, till bean mixture is piping hot. Makes about 6 servings.

SMOKY BEAN SKILLET

½ cup finely chopped onion
¼ cup chopped green pepper
2 tablespoons salad oil
1 12-ounce package (8) link sausages, cut in 1-inch pieces
1 15-ounce can (1⅔ cups) butter beans, drained
2 1-pound cans (4 cups) pork and beans in tomato sauce
¼ cup barbecue sauce

In large skillet cook chopped onion and green pepper in oil till tender but not brown. Stir in remaining ingredients. Cover and simmer 15 to 20 minutes, stirring occasionally. Serve piping hot. Makes 6 to 8 servings.

RANCHO BEAN CASSEROLE

Hearty main dish with spunky seasoning—

½ pound ground beef
. . .
½ envelope or can (¼ cup) dry onion-soup mix
½ cup water
⅓ cup catsup
1 tablespoon prepared mustard
1 1-pound can (2 cups) pork and beans in tomato sauce
1 1-pound can (2 cups) dark red kidney beans, drained

Brown ground beef. Stir in remaining ingredients. Pour into a 1½-quart casserole. Bake covered in moderate oven (350°) for 1 hour. Makes 6 to 8 servings.

POTLUCK BEAN BAKE

1 1-pound can (2 cups) beans in barbecue sauce
1 8-ounce can (1 cup) Limas with ham
1 1-pound can (2 cups) cut green beans, drained
1 teaspoon instant minced onion

Combine ingredients in 1½-quart casserole. Stir to mix. Bake in moderate oven (350°) for about 1½ hours. Let stand 10 minutes before serving. Makes 8 servings.

Here's homespun Yankee cooking at its best—Old-time Baked Beans! The secret of the wonderful flavor is a little molasses and salt pork, then slow and easy cooking (your oven does the work). You'll agree with the Pilgrims—mighty good fare!

OLD-TIME BAKED BEANS

1 pound (2 cups) dry navy beans
1½ quarts cold water
1 teaspoon salt

. . .

½ cup brown sugar
1 teaspoon salt
1 teaspoon dry mustard
¼ cup molasses
¼ pound salt pork
1 medium onion, sliced

Rinse beans; add to cold water. Bring to boiling; simmer 2 minutes; remove from heat; cover, let stand 1 hour. (Or, add beans to water; let soak overnight.)

Add 1 teaspoon salt to beans and soaking water; cover; simmer till *tender,* about 1 hour. Drain, reserving liquid. Measure ¾ cup bean liquid. Combine with sugar, salt, mustard, and molasses. Cut salt pork in half; score one half, set aside. Grind or thin-slice remainder.

In 2-quart bean pot or casserole, alternate layers of beans, onion, ground salt pork, and sugar mixture. Repeat layers. Top with scored salt pork. Cover; bake in slow oven (300°) for 5 to 7 hours, adding more liquid if needed. Makes 8 servings.

BEAN-POT LIMAS

1 pound (2½ cups) large dry Limas
6 cups water

• • •

¼ pound salt pork
2 cups hot bean liquor
1 medium onion, sliced
2 teaspoons salt
½ teaspoon dry mustard
⅓ cup dark molasses
⅓ cup chili sauce
1 tablespoon vinegar

Rinse beans, soak in 6 cups water overnight. Don't drain. Cover; simmer over low heat (do not boil) until just tender, about 30 minutes. Drain, reserving bean liquor.

Cut salt pork in half; grind one piece, score the other in squares. Combine all ingredients but the scored salt pork. Pour into 2-quart bean pot or casserole. Top with scored salt-pork slice. Cover and bake in slow oven (300°) for 2½ hours, uncovering the last 30 minutes of baking time. (If necessary, add additional bean liquor or hot water during baking.) Makes 8 servings.

PINK BEANS SUPREME

In barbecue season, soak the beans the night before, then finish on the grill—

1 pound (2½ cups) large dry Limas

• • •

2 cups chopped onions
¼ cup butter or margarine
½ cup sliced mushrooms
2 tablespoons paprika

• • •

2 cups dairy sour cream
1 teaspoon salt

Rinse Limas, then cover with 6 cups cold water and bring to boiling. Simmer 2 minutes and remove from heat. Cover and let stand 1 hour. Add 2 teaspoons salt to beans (don't drain); bring to boiling, reduce heat, cover and simmer mixture for 45 to 60 minutes or till tender. Drain.

Cook onions in butter till tender. Add mushrooms and paprika; cook 5 minutes longer. Stir in beans, sour cream, and salt; heat through, stirring now and then. If desired, garnish with parsley. Serves 12.

FIESTA LIMAS

Cook 2½ cups fresh shelled *or* two 10-ounce packages frozen green Limas and 1 cup sliced celery in boiling (unsalted) water till tender; drain.

Meanwhile melt 2 tablespoons butter or margarine; blend in 2 tablespoons all-purpose flour. Stir in 1 cup milk. Cook and stir till thick. Season with ½ teaspoon salt and dash pepper. Add ½ cup finely diced sharp process American cheese and 1 tablespoon chopped canned pimiento. Stir in hot Limas; mix well. Makes 6 servings.

SWEDISH BROWN BEANS

Rinse 1 pound (2¼ cups) Swedish brown beans; drain. Add 5 cups cold water; cover and let stand overnight. (Or bring water and beans slowly to boiling; reduce heat and simmer 2 minutes; cover; let stand 1 hour.)

Add 3 inches stick cinnamon and 1½ teaspoons salt. Cover and simmer 1 hour or till beans start to get tender. Add ⅓ cup brown sugar and ¼ cup vinegar. Cook uncovered, 45 minutes longer or till beans are tender and liquid is nice consistency. Stir now and then. Add 2 tablespoons dark corn syrup. Makes 6 servings.

MEXICAN BEAN CASSEROLE

1 6-ounce package (about 4 cups) corn chips
2 cups shredded sharp process American cheese
1 15-ounce can (1⅔ cups) chili with beans
1 15-ounce can (1⅔ cups) enchilada sauce
1 8-ounce can tomato sauce
1 tablespoon instant minced onion
1 cup dairy sour cream

Reserve 1 *cup* of the corn chips and ½ *cup* of the cheese. Combine remaining chips and cheese with the chili, sauces, and onion. Pour into 1½-quart casserole. Bake uncovered in moderate oven (375°) for 20 minutes or till thoroughly heated. Spread top with sour cream; sprinkle with reserved cheese. Ring remaining corn chips around edge. Bake 5 minutes longer. Serves 6.

DELUXE LIMAS

Easy fix-up for Limas—

Into bowl empty one 10-ounce package (2 cups) frozen green Limas. Pour boiling water over and break the beans apart. Drain well.

Blend together 1 can condensed cheese soup and ½ cup milk; add drained Limas, ¾ cup sliced celery, and ¼ cup snipped parsley. Stir in *half* of a 3½-ounce can French-fried onions. Bake at 350° for 35 minutes. Border casserole with remaining onions. Bake 10 minutes more or till onions are crispy. Makes 6 servings.

QUICK CREOLE LIMAS

Cook 2 tablespoons chopped onion in 1 tablespoon butter or margarine till tender. Add one 1-pound can (2 cups) tomatoes, 1 teaspoon sugar, ½ teaspoon salt, and dash pepper. Simmer 15 minutes; stir occasionally. Brown ½ cup soft bread crumbs in 1 tablespoon butter or margarine. Add one 1-pound can Limas, drained, and the bread crumbs to tomato mixture. Heat through. Makes 5 or 6 servings.

SAUCY VEGETABLE TRIO

Tasty combination—perfect for a buffet—

For sauce combine 1 cup mayonnaise or salad dressing and 2 hard-cooked eggs, chopped. Blend in 3 tablespoons lemon juice, 2 tablespoons minced onion, 1 teaspoon Worcestershire sauce, 1 teaspoon prepared mustard, ¼ teaspoon garlic salt, and dash bottled hot pepper sauce. Heat and stir over *low heat* just till heated through.

Cook according to package directions: one 10-ounce package frozen French-style green beans, one 10-ounce package frozen peas, and one 10-ounce package frozen baby Limas. Drain vegetables and mix. Pour hot sauce over. Makes 8 to 10 servings.

SAVORY TOMATO-LIMAS

Old-fashioned fare with a Mexican accent!—

2 cups large dry Limas
6 cups water
¼ pound salt pork, cut in ½-inch cubes

. . .

1 medium onion, sliced
1 clove garlic, minced
2 tablespoons butter or margarine
1 tablespoon prepared mustard
1 teaspoon Worcestershire sauce
1 teaspoon salt
1 teaspoon chili powder
1 10½-ounce can condensed tomato soup
¼ cup vinegar

Rinse Limas; cover with cold water and bring to boiling. Simmer 2 minutes; remove from heat. Cover and let stand 1 hour. Add salt pork to beans (don't drain). Cover; cook slowly until tender, about 1½ to 2 hours. Drain, reserving 1½ cups liquid. Place beans in a 2-quart casserole.

Cook onion and garlic in butter till golden. Add bean liquid and remaining ingredients. Pour over Limas. Bake uncovered in hot oven (400°) for 30 minutes. Stir once or twice while baking. Serves 8.

GREEN LIMAS WITH BACON DRESSING

This same flavorful dressing is tasty with spinach and other greens—

3 slices bacon, cut in 1-inch pieces
2 teaspoons finely chopped onion
1/3 cup tomato juice
1 teaspoon vinegar
1/4 teaspoon celery seed
Dash pepper

. . .

1 10-ounce package frozen Limas, cooked and drained

Brown bacon lightly in skillet. Add onion and cook over low heat until tender but not brown. Add remaining ingredients except beans, and simmer 5 minutes. Serve over hot Limas. Makes 4 servings.

COPENHAGEN LIMAS

Cook one 10-ounce package frozen Limas in *unsalted* water according to package directions; drain. Heat 1/4 cup milk with 1/4 cup crumbled blue cheese, stirring till cheese melts. Add cooked beans.

Combine 1/4 cup fine dry bread crumbs and 1 tablespoon butter or margarine, melted. Stir over medium heat till golden brown. Turn beans into serving bowl; sprinkle with crumbs. Makes 4 servings.

GREEN BEANS ALMOND

Cook 1/4 cup slivered blanched almonds in 1/4 cup butter or margarine over low heat till golden; stir occasionally. Remove from heat; add 1/4 teaspoon salt and 1 to 2 teaspoons lemon juice.

Pour over 2 cups hot, cooked, drained, French-style green beans. Makes 4 servings.

GREEN BEANS BEARNAISE

Diced ham imparts wonderful smoky flavor to green beans—fresh, frozen or canned—

1 pound fresh green beans, French-cut *or* 1 9-ounce package frozen *or* 1 1-pound can (2 cups) French-style green beans

. . .

1 tablespoon butter or margarine
1/2 cup finely diced fully cooked ham
1 small clove garlic, minced
1/2 teaspoon salt
Dash pepper
1 medium tomato, cut in wedges

Cook fresh or frozen green beans in small amount of boiling water till just tender; drain. Or heat canned beans and drain.

Melt butter in saucepan; add ham and garlic; cook till garlic is softened. Stir in beans, salt, and pepper. Top with tomato; cover, heat through. Makes 4 servings.

It's simple to make elegant Frenched green beans with a bean slicer. Snip ends off beans. Remove strings. Pull bean through slicer. If you have no tool, hold bean on cutting board; with knife, zip diagonally end to end.

Sesame French-cut Beans: Cook one 9-ounce package frozen French-style green beans according to package directions; drain well.

Melt 2 tablespoons butter or margarine in a skillet. Add 2 teaspoons sesame seeds and cook till light brown. Stir in 1 tablespoon wine vinegar and 1 teaspoon soy sauce; simmer 2 to 3 minutes. Pour over green beans and toss lightly. Makes 4 servings.

BEAN SUCCOTASH

Here's a grand way with green beans! Just add polka dots of green pepper and corn —so pretty and delicious, too.

Cook ¼ cup chopped onion and ¼ cup chopped green pepper in 2 tablespoons butter or margarine until tender but not brown. Drain one 1-pound can French-style green beans and one 12-ounce can whole kernel corn. Add to skillet. Season with salt and pepper. Cover; heat through. Garnish with pepper rings. Serves 6 or 7.

EASY BEAN RELISH

Cool and refreshing! The flavor gets even better as the relish stands, so make it the night before. It's a perfect complement for a Dutch lunch of cold cuts, cheeses, and assorted breads—

Combine liquid from one 1-pound can whole green beans with ⅓ cup vinegar, 2 tablespoons sugar, 1 teaspoon dill seed, 1 teaspoon mixed pickling spices, and 1 teaspoon salt. Simmer 5 minutes. Add beans; heat through. Cool in liquid; drain. Mix beans, 1 onion (cut in thin rings), and 1 tablespoon salad oil. Chill.

CREAMY GREEN BEANS

The easy sauce is cream cheese. Nice for fresh or canned green beans, too—

Cook one 9-ounce package frozen green beans, following label directions; drain.

Soften one 3-ounce package cream cheese; blend in 1 tablespoon milk, ¼ teaspoon celery seed, and ¼ teaspoon salt. Add to beans and heat through. Makes 4 servings.

ITALIAN GREEN BEANS

In skillet, lightly brown 2 to 3 tablespoons slivered blanched almonds in 3 tablespoons butter or margarine. Stir occasionally. Meanwhile, cook two 9-ounce packages frozen Italian green beans according to package directions; drain well.

Place green beans in warmed serving dish; pour toasted almond and butter mixture over. Toss gently. Makes 6 servings.

HERBED GREEN BEANS

The flavor bouquet here is delightful, thanks to garlic, basil, and rosemary in just the right amounts—

1 pound fresh green beans, cut in 1-inch lengths (about 3 cups)*

• • •

2 to 3 tablespoons butter or margarine
½ cup chopped onion
¼ cup chopped celery
1 clove garlic, minced
¼ teaspoon basil
¼ teaspoon rosemary

Cook beans, covered, in small amount boiling salted water until almost tender, about 10 minutes; drain. Stir in remaining ingredients. Cover; cook 10 minutes longer or until beans are tender. Serves 4 to 6.

*For canned beans, drain; add remaining ingredients and heat over low heat.

DUTCH GREEN BEANS

1 medium onion, sliced and separated in rings
3 tablespoons butter or margarine
2 9-ounce packages frozen French-style green beans
⅓ cup water
1 teaspoon salt

Cook onion in butter until tender, but not brown. Add beans and water; sprinkle with salt. Cover and bring to boiling; reduce heat and simmer 5 to 7 minutes or till just tender. Makes 8 servings.

SNAPPY GREEN BEANS

4 slices bacon
¼ cup chopped onion
1 to 2 tablespoons tarragon vinegar
2 cups hot, drained green beans

Fry bacon till crisp; drain. Cook onion in 2 tablespoons of the bacon fat till tender. Add vinegar. Season with ½ teaspoon salt, dash pepper. Pour over hot beans. Crumble bacon atop. Makes 3 or 4 servings.

CARAWAY GREEN BEANS

2 tablespoons all-purpose flour
½ cup dairy sour cream
2 tablespoons finely chopped onion
1 tablespoon sugar
½ teaspoon salt
Dash pepper
Dash nutmeg
½ cup milk
¼ pound caraway Cheddar cheese, crumbled (1 cup)

• • •

2 9-ounce packages frozen *or* 2 1-pound cans (4 cups) French-style green beans, cooked and drained

Blend flour with sour cream. Stir in remaining ingredients except green beans. Heat and stir just until cheese melts. Stir in hot drained beans. Heat through. Sprinkle with nutmeg. Makes 6 to 8 servings.

GREEN BEANS WITH CREAMY DILL SAUCE

1 4-ounce package pimiento whipped cream cheese
1 tablespoon light cream
½ teaspoon dill weed
¼ teaspoon salt

• • •

1 9-ounce package frozen French-style green beans

Blend together cream cheese, cream, dill weed, and salt. Cook beans according to package directions; drain. Pour sauce over; toss lightly to melt cheese. Serves 4.

FIESTA WAX BEANS

1 1-pound can (2 cups) cut wax beans
⅔ cup diced celery
2 tablespoons butter or margarine
1 chicken bouillon cube
¼ cup chili sauce

Drain beans, *reserving ¼ cup liquid.* Cook celery in butter until tender. Add reserved bean liquid and bouillon cube. Simmer till dissolved. Stir in chili sauce and beans. Heat through. Makes 4 servings.

GREEN BEANS SUPREME

Add a subtle sauce of sour cream and a touch of lemon—green beans go gala!—

½ cup sliced onion
2 tablespoons butter or margarine
2 tablespoons all-purpose flour
1 teaspoon salt
¼ teaspoon pepper
½ teaspoon grated lemon peel
1 tablespoon snipped parsley
5 cups drained, cooked, or canned green beans
1 cup dairy sour cream
½ cup shredded sharp process American cheese
2 tablespoons butter or margarine, melted
½ cup dry bread crumbs

Cook onion in 2 tablespoons butter till tender but not brown. Add flour, salt, pepper, lemon peel, and parsley; cook and stir till mixture bubbles. Blend in sour cream. Add beans; heat through, stirring. Turn into 10x6x1½-inch baking dish. Top with cheese. Combine melted butter and bread crumbs; sprinkle over beans. Broil just till cheese melts and crumbs brown. Serves 8.

BEAN 'N ONION BAKE

2 9-ounce packages frozen cut green beans
1 8-ounce can (1 cup) small white onions, drained
4 slices bacon
1 tablespoon all-purpose flour
½ cup tomato juice
1 cup shredded sharp process American cheese
1 tablespoon prepared mustard

Cook beans according to package directions; drain, *reserving ¼ cup liquid.* Arrange beans and onions in 10x6x1½-inch baking dish. Cook bacon till crisp; remove and crumble. Blend flour into 1 tablespoon of the bacon drippings. Add tomato juice and bean liquid. Cook, stirring constantly, till mixture thickens. Add cheese and mustard; stir till cheese melts. Pour over vegetables; mix gently. Sprinkle with bacon. Bake in a moderate oven (375°) for 20 minutes. Serves 6.

BUFFET VEGETABLE BAKE

Serve this colorful casserole next time you entertain—it's bound to be your most asked-for recipe! You can do all the fixing ahead of time, then refrigerate until time to heat in the oven—

2 10-ounce packages frozen mixed peas and carrots
1 9-ounce package frozen whole green beans
1 5-ounce can water chestnuts, drained and sliced
1 3-ounce can (⅔ cup) broiled sliced mushrooms, drained

• • •

1 10½-ounce can condensed cream of mushroom soup
3 to 4 tablespoons cooking sherry
1 teaspoon Worcestershire sauce
Dash bottled hot pepper sauce
2 cups shredded sharp process American cheese
¼ cup rich round cracker crumbs

Cook peas and carrots, and beans till just barely tender; drain. Combine with water chestnuts and mushrooms.

Combine remaining ingredients, except crumbs, for sauce. Toss with vegetables. Turn into 2-quart casserole.

Bake uncovered in moderate oven (350°) for 40 to 45 minutes till hot and bubbly. Stir occasionally. Sprinkle with crumbs just before serving. Serves 10 to 12.

ELEGANT GREEN BEANS

4 cups cooked or canned green beans
¼ cup chopped onion
3 tablespoons butter or margarine
2 tablespoons all-purpose flour
2 tablespoons sugar
2 tablespoons vinegar
¼ cup snipped parsley
1 cup dairy sour cream
3 slices bacon, cooked crisp

Drain beans, reserving *1 cup* liquid. Cook onion in butter till soft. Stir in flour. Stir in bean liquid, sugar, vinegar, and parsley. Cook, stirring constantly, till thickened. Add sour cream and pour over the beans; heat through, but do not boil. Crumble bacon over top. Makes 6 to 8 servings.

GREEN BEANS CAESAR

Nice piquant flavor. In a toot? Use ready-made croutons from your grocery—

1 cup bread cubes
2 tablespoons salad oil
1 tablespoon salad oil
1 tablespoon vinegar
1 teaspoon instant minced onion
¼ teaspoon salt
1 1-pound can (2 cups) cut green beans, drained
2 tablespoons shredded Parmesan cheese

Brown bread cubes lightly in the *2 tablespoons* salad oil. Remove from pan. In same skillet, mix 1 tablespoon oil, the vinegar, onion and salt. Stir in beans; heat through. Add toasted bread cubes and Parmesan cheese. Toss gently. Makes 4 servings.

DILLY GREEN BEANS

1 cup chopped onion
¼ cup butter or margarine
4 cups whole fresh green beans, *or* 2 9-ounce packages frozen whole green beans, cooked and drained
1 teaspoon salt
Dash pepper
1 tablespoon snipped fresh dill *or* 1½ teaspoons dill seed
2 hard-cooked eggs

Cook onion in butter till golden. Add hot green beans, salt, pepper, and dill; toss lightly. Top with chopped egg whites and sieved egg yolks. Makes 8 servings.

SWEET-SOUR GREEN BEANS

Easy variety for green beans—

1 1-pound can (2 cups) green beans
3 slices bacon, diced
3 tablespoons sweet-pickle juice

Drain beans, cook liquid until only ⅓ cup remains. Fry bacon till crisp; drain.

Add beans, bacon, and pickle juice to the hot bean liquid. Simmer to blend the flavors; about 15 minutes. Makes 4 or 5 servings.

GREEN BEANS ORIENTAL

2 teaspoons instant minced onion
2 tablespoons white wine vinegar
3 slices bacon
1 tablespoon sugar
½ teaspoon salt
1 1-pound can (2 cups) cut green beans, drained
1 1-pound can (2 cups) bean sprouts, drained

Combine onion and vinegar; let stand 5 minutes. Cook bacon till crisp; remove and crumble. To bacon drippings, add vinegar mixture, sugar, and salt. Stir in beans and bean sprouts; heat through. Serve topped with crumbled bacon. Makes 6 to 8 servings.

SAVORY GREEN BEANS

2 1-pound cans (4 cups) green beans, drained
1 teaspoon summer savory
2 tablespoons finely chopped canned pimiento
⅓ cup butter or margarine
½ teaspoon salt
Dash pepper

Combine beans with remaining ingredients. Heat slowly; stir often. Makes 6 servings.

MUSTARD GREEN BEANS

4 cups fresh green beans
1 tablespoon butter or margarine
1 tablespoon all-purpose flour
1 tablespoon prepared mustard
½ teaspoon salt
1 cup milk
2 egg yolks, beaten
3 slices bacon, crisp cooked

Cook green beans in a small amount of boiling salted water for 20 to 30 minutes or till tender; drain. Melt butter; blend in flour, mustard, and salt. Add milk all at once. Cook stirring constantly, till thick. Add small amount of sauce to beaten egg yolks; return to remaining sauce and cook, stirring constantly, about 1 minute. Pour over beans. Spoon into serving dish. Crumble bacon over the top. Makes 6 to 8 servings.

beets

Originally, the beet plant grew wild in the Caspian Sea region. Then for many centuries, beets were cultivated for their succulent green tops. Now the sweet delicious beet root provides the primary produce. First cousins of our red garden beet are sugar beets, cultivated for sugar production, and Swiss chard, which is used as spinach.

You'll find early or new beets in your market, usually in bunches, with or without tops. The vegetable crisper in your refrigerator keeps these beets fresh. The fall or late crop of beets is usually sold without tops and is suitable for longer storage during the winter months—keep these beets in a dry place at a cool temperature.

Look for smooth, rounded beets without ridges or blemishes—the ones shown at left are of prime quality. Beets of medium size are least likely to be tough or woody. Wilted or damaged leaves do not necessarily mean inferior beets, since beet tops deteriorate quickly without immediately affecting the beets themselves.

Often beet tops are removed from young beets and sold as greens. Looks are important here—you'll want young tender leaves that are fresh green and not wilted. Avoid coarse, heavy-veined leaves as they are generally tough. Wash leaves carefully; drain on paper towels. Store wrapped in a plastic bag or clear plastic wrap in the vegetable crisper of the refrigerator.

BEETS IN SOUR CREAM

There's just enough savory sauce to give beets a rosy glow. Delicious! For garnish, top with additional sour cream and chopped green onions—

For the easy sauce, combine 1/4 cup dairy sour cream, 1 tablespoon vinegar, 1 teaspoon minced green onions, 3/4 teaspoon sugar, 1/2 teaspoon salt, and dash cayenne. Add sauce to 2 1/2 cups halved cooked beets, drained. Heat slowly, stirring now and then to coat each beat half evenly. (Do not boil.) Makes 4 or 5 servings.

BEETS 'N ORANGE

The pretty glaze is gently flavored with orange juice; orange sections are trim—

In saucepan mix 3 tablespoons sugar, 1 1/2 teaspoons cornstarch, and 1 teaspoon salt. Add 1 tablespoon butter. Blend over low heat. Slowly stir in 1/2 cup orange juice. Cook and stir till sauce thickens. Pour over 8 to 10 drained hot cooked beets—whole, sliced, diced, or julienne-style. Serves 4.

NIPPY BEETS

These spicy beets add the sparkle of spring to any meal! The good honey-mustard sauce makes them almost deviled. They're a natural to serve with baked ham. Or for a speedy supper, team them with broiled Canadian bacon slices—

In saucepan blend 3 tablespoons butter or margarine, 2 tablespoons prepared mustard, 1 tablespoon honey, and 1 teaspoon Worcestershire sauce. Add salt to taste. Heat mixture just to boiling; remove saucepan from heat.

Spoon sauce over 2 cups hot drained cooked beets; stir to glaze. Serves 4.

HARVARD BEETS

1 1-pound can (2 cups) diced beets
2 tablespoons sugar
1 tablespoon cornstarch
1/4 teaspoon salt
1/4 cup vinegar
2 tablespoons butter or margarine

Drain beets, *reserving 1/3 cup liquid.* In saucepan combine sugar, cornstarch, and salt. Stir in reserved beet liquid, vinegar, and butter. Cook and stir till mixture thickens. Add beets; heat through. Serves 4.

CANDIED BEETS

Drain one 1-pound can (2 cups) sliced beets, *reserving 2 tablespoons liquid.* In saucepan combine the drained beets, reserved liquid, 1/4 cup currant jelly, 2 tablespoons vinegar, dash salt, and dash cloves. Cover and simmer 10 minutes. Mix 1 teaspoon cornstarch and 1 teaspoon water; stir into beet mixture. Cook till mixture bubbles. Add 1 tablespoon butter. Serves 4.

BEET-ONION MEDLEY

Drain one 1-pound can (2 cups) sliced beets, *reserving 2 tablespoons juice.* In skillet or saucepan, melt 2 tablespoons butter or margarine; add the drained beets, reserved 2 tablespoons juice, 1 cup thin onion slices, and 1/4 cup chopped celery.

Cover; cook over low heat till onion and celery are tender, about 12 minutes. Season with salt and pepper. Sprinkle with 1 tablespoon snipped parsley. Serves 4.

CRANBERRY-ORANGE BEETS

1 cup cranberry-juice cocktail
1 tablespoon cornstarch
1 tablespoon sugar
2 1-pound cans sliced beets drained
1/4 teaspoon grated orange peel

In saucepan gradually stir cranberry juice into cornstarch, sugar, and dash salt. Cook and stir over medium heat till mixture thickens and boils. Add beets and orange peel. Simmer, uncovered, 10 minutes. Serves 4.

ORANGE-GLAZED BEETS

This easy-to-do glaze gives beets a flavor that's fresh as spring!—

1 1/2 pounds fresh or 1 1-pound can (about 2 cups) small whole beets, drained
3 tablespoons butter or margarine
1/4 cup orange marmalade
1 tablespoon orange juice

Cut off all but 1 inch of stems and roots of fresh beets; do not pare. Cook, covered, in boiling salted water about 35 minutes or until tender. Drain and peel.

Melt butter in skillet; stir in marmalade and orange juice. Add the cooked or the drained canned beets. Cook and stir over low heat till beets are heated through and glazed, about 6 to 8 minutes.

Garnish with thin slices of orange, if desired. Makes 4 servings.

BEET 'N APPLE SKILLET

There's nice mellow flavor here. Serve this dish along with roast pork—

Cook 1/2 cup chopped onion in 1/4 cup butter till tender. Add 6 medium beets, cooked and sliced, or one 1-pound can sliced beets, drained, and 2 medium apples, chopped. Cover and cook slowly till apples are tender. Add 1/2 teaspoon salt and dash nutmeg.

BEETS WITH PINEAPPLE

2 tablespoons brown sugar
1 tablespoon cornstarch
1/4 teaspoon salt
1 9-ounce can (1 cup) pineapple tidbits
1 tablespoon butter or margarine
1 tablespoon lemon juice
1 1-pound can (2 cups) sliced beets, drained

Combine brown sugar, cornstarch, and salt in saucepan. Stir in pineapple (with syrup). Cook, stirring constantly, till mixture thickens and bubbles. Add butter, lemon juice, and drained beets. Heat through, for about 5 minutes. Makes 4 servings.

broccoli

The most familiar form of this sophisticated cabbage family member is the "sprouting" or Italian broccoli. However, a long-season-type of cauliflower resembling broccoli is still available in some markets. When buying broccoli, look for firm, tender stalks with green to purplish-green buds which are tightly closed and form compact clusters. The size of heads varies but does not affect the eating quality. Beware of quantities of yellow or brown flowers inside the buds—this indicates older broccoli which may be tough. Be extra careful in storing broccoli, as it tends to be one of the more highly perishable vegetables. Wrap well in foil or clear plastic wrap and refrigerate at a low temperature to prevent undesirable yellowing of the buds.

To prepare broccoli, trim off a bit of the stem, but do not remove the stems, for the entire stalk, buds, and leaves are edible. The raw flowerets are also delicious when served on a relish tray with a flavorful dip or tossed in a green salad.

Although Thomas Jefferson succeeded in growing broccoli from seed in the late 1700s, the crop remained relatively unknown in America until 1920. At this time, some trial fields were planted in California. The cool months provided an excellent climate and this lush vegetable was soon savored from coast to coast.

BROCCOLI ITALIENNE

2 10-ounce packages frozen broccoli spears *or* 2 pounds fresh broccoli
½ teaspoon oregano, crushed
½ cup mayonnaise or salad dressing
¼ cup shredded sharp process cheese
1 tablespoon milk

Cook broccoli till tender in boiling salted water to which oregano has been added; drain. In top of double boiler, mix mayonnaise, cheese, and milk; heat over hot, not boiling water, stirring till cheese melts and mixture is hot. Serve with broccoli. Serves 6.

BROCCOLI-CORN BAKE

1 10-ounce package frozen chopped broccoli, thawed
1 1-pound can cream-style corn
¼ cup cracker crumbs
1 beaten egg
2 tablespoons butter, melted
1 tablespoon instant minced onion
½ teaspoon salt
Dash pepper
¼ cup cracker crumbs
2 tablespoons butter, melted

Combine first 8 ingredients in a 1½-quart casserole. Blend ¼ cup cracker crumbs and 2 tablespoons butter; sprinkle over top. Bake in 350° oven 45 minutes. Serves 6.

BROCCOLI CASSEROLE

2 tablespoons butter, melted
2 tablespoons all-purpose flour
1 3-ounce package cream cheese, softened
¼ cup crumbled blue cheese (1 ounce)
1 cup milk
2 10-ounce packages frozen chopped broccoli, cooked and drained
⅓ cup rich round crackers, crushed (about 10)

In a large saucepan blend butter, flour, and cheeses. Add milk; cook and stir till mixture boils. Stir in cooked broccoli. Place in a 1-quart casserole; top with cracker crumbs. Bake at 350° for 30 minutes. Serves 8 to 10.

CASSEROLE A LA KING

1 10½-ounce can chicken a la king
1 10½-ounce can condensed cream of celery soup
¾ cup shredded sharp process cheese
1 teaspoon prepared mustard
½ teaspoon Worcestershire sauce
½ teaspoon curry powder
2 cups fine noodles
1 10-ounce package frozen broccoli spears

Heat chicken, soup, cheese, and seasonings till cheese is melted, stirring frequently. Meanwhile cook noodles in boiling *unsalted* water till tender; cook broccoli in boiling salted water till just tender.

Drain noodles and broccoli. Place noodles in greased 10x6x1½-inch baking dish. Arrange broccoli spears atop; pour chicken mixture over. Bake in moderate oven (375°) for 10 to 15 minutes. Makes 4 servings.

BROCCOLI PARMESAN

Cook two 10-ounce packages frozen broccoli spears *or* 2 pounds fresh broccoli in boiling *unsalted* water till tender; drain well.

Melt 2 tablespoons butter or margarine in saucepan; add ¼ cup chopped onion and cook till tender but not brown. Blend in one 10½-ounce can condensed cream of chicken soup, ⅔ cup milk, and ⅓ cup grated Parmesan cheese. Heat thoroughly. Serve sauce over hot broccoli. Serves 6 to 8.

BROCCOLI WITH SHRIMP

1 4-ounce carton chive whipped cream cheese
¼ cup milk
1 10-ounce can frozen condensed cream of shrimp soup
2 teaspoons lemon juice
2 10-ounce packages frozen broccoli spears, cooked and drained
Toasted slivered almonds

In saucepan blend cream cheese and milk. Add shrimp soup; heat and stir until soup is thawed and mixture is smooth. Heat through; add lemon juice. Pour over broccoli and sprinkle with almonds. Serves 6.

BROCCOLI SOUFFLE

1 10-ounce package frozen chopped broccoli
2 tablespoons butter or margarine
2 tablespoons all-purpose flour
½ teaspoon salt
½ cup milk
¼ cup grated Parmesan cheese
4 egg yolks
4 stiff-beaten egg whites
Mushroom Sauce

Cook broccoli following package directions. Drain *very thoroughly*. (Chop large pieces.) Add butter to broccoli; cook and stir over high heat till butter is melted and moisture is evaporated. Reserve 2 tablespoons broccoli. Blend in flour and salt; add milk all at once. Cook and stir over medium heat till mixture thickens and bubbles. Remove from heat; stir in grated Parmesan cheese.

Beat egg yolks till thick and lemon-colored. Add broccoli to egg yolks, stirring constantly; pour over egg whites; fold together thoroughly. Pour into *ungreased* 1-quart souffle dish. Bake in a moderate oven (350°) for 20 minutes; ring souffle top with reserved broccoli. Bake 15 minutes longer or till knife inserted comes out clean. Serve with Mushroom Sauce. Makes 4 to 6 servings.

MUSHROOM SAUCE

Lightly brown 1 pint sliced fresh mushrooms *or* one 6-ounce can broiled sliced mushrooms, drained in ¼ cup butter or margarine, melted. Blend in 2 tablespoons all-purpose flour, and dash *each* salt and pepper. Add 1 cup water and 1 chicken bouillon cube; cook and stir till sauce is boiling. Stir in 1 tablespoon chopped pimiento; cook 1 to 2 minutes longer. Serve piping hot.

A golden crowned souffle that puffs up elegantly into an airy treat is a perfect way to dress up everyday chopped broccoli. Your guests will delight to its fluffy texture and luscious flavor. Creamy-good Mushroom Sauce adds just the right zest.

brussels sprouts

Tender cooked Brussels sprouts are prepared by a French method known as a la Polonaise—a coating of sieved egg yolk, parsley, browned butter and crumbs.

Belgium claims the fame for naming Brussels sprouts since this peculiar member of the cabbage tribe has been grown in that country for hundreds of years. The plants grow about two feet tall and have many tiny heads or immature buds that form along the stems. Protecting these tiny heads are small cabbage-like leaves tightly wrapped around each other. Each sprout is usually one to two inches in diameter. Freshly cooked, they're a nutritionist's delight with abundant amounts of vitamin C, vitamin A, and very few calories.

When buying Brussels sprouts, choose firm compact heads with bright green color. Wilted or yellow leaves indicate poor quality. Sprouts are a highly perishable vegetable so should be stored in a refrigerator crisper until they're used.

BRUSSELS SPROUTS POLONAISE

Elite "little cabbages" with buttered crumbs—

2 pounds Brussels sprouts (about 8 cups)
¼ cup butter or margarine
¼ cup fine dry bread crumbs
1 hard-cooked egg yolk, sieved
2 tablespoons snipped parsley

Cut very large Brussels sprouts in half; cook sprouts, covered, in boiling salted water for 12 to 15 minutes or till just tender; drain. Heat butter in small saucepan or skillet till it begins to brown; add crumbs, egg yolk, and parsley. Spoon mixture over sprouts; toss lightly. Serves 6 to 8.

BLUE CHEESED SPROUTS

2 pints fresh Brussels sprouts *or* 2 10-ounce packages frozen Brussels sprouts

. . .

2 tablespoons (½ ounce) blue cheese, crumbled
¼ cup butter or margarine

Wash and trim fresh sprouts; cook covered in boiling salted water for about 15 minutes or till tender. Or cook frozen Brussels sprouts according to package directions. Drain thoroughly. Melt butter and blend in blue cheese. Toss with hot drained sprouts. Serves 6.

BRUSSELS SPROUTS ROYALE

Thin slices of crunchy water chestnuts contrast with tender cooked sprouts—

2 10-ounce packages frozen Brussels sprouts
¼ cup butter or margarine
1 5-ounce can water chestnuts, drained and sliced
¼ cup snipped parsley

Thaw Brussels sprouts enough to separate; halve larger sprouts. Cook according to package directions. Melt butter and add water chestnuts and parsley. Heat thoroughly and toss with cooked sprouts. Serves 6.

BRUSSELS SPROUTS SOUFFLE

Cheddar cheese complements the flavor—

¼ cup butter or margarine
¼ cup all-purpose flour
½ teaspoon salt
1 cup milk
4 egg yolks
1 cup shredded Cheddar cheese
1 10-ounce package frozen Brussels sprouts, cooked, drained, and finely chopped (about 2 cups)
4 egg whites

Melt butter and blend in the flour and salt. Add milk all at once and cook quickly till mixture thickens, stirring constantly. Beat egg yolks till thick and lemon-colored. Blend some of the hot mixture into egg yolks; return to hot mixture and stir rapidly.

Stir in cheese and finely chopped sprouts. Remove pan from heat. Beat egg whites until stiff but not dry; fold into hot mixture. Turn into an *ungreased* 2-quart souffle dish. Bake in a moderate oven (350°) for 40 minutes or till knife inserted comes out clean. Makes 4 to 6 servings.

BRUSSELS SPROUTS AND MUSHROOMS

1 pint fresh Brussels sprouts*
1 teaspoon salt
4 cups cold water
1 cup boiling water
1 pint fresh mushrooms, sliced
3 tablespoons butter or margarine
Dash pepper
2 tablespoons chopped canned pimiento

Wash and trim sprouts. Put in saucepan with 1 teaspoon salt and 4 cups cold water; soak 30 minutes. Drain and rinse well. Put in saucepan with 1 cup boiling water. Cook, covered for 15 minutes, or till just tender. Drain. Meanwhile, cook mushrooms in butter till tender and golden brown. Add to sprouts and season with salt and pepper to taste. Put in serving dish and garnish with chopped pimiento. Makes 6 servings.

*One 10-ounce package frozen Brussels sprouts may be substituted for fresh. Cook as directed on package; drain and use as above.

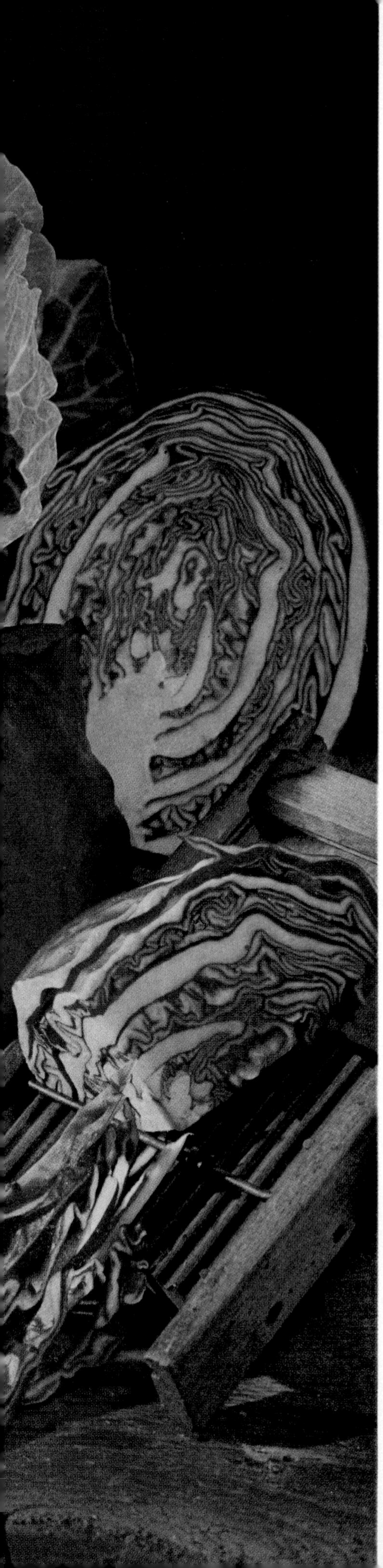

cabbage

Dedicated researchers tell us that cabbage is one of the first recorded vegetables, that it was important over 5,000 years ago. Though its exact origin is still speculative, we're told it was once esteemed so highly in Egypt that it was glorified in certain worship ceremonies.

Our pioneers held cabbage in high esteem too, but for survival, for a food crop to depend on. Cabbage defied poor soil conditions. As gardening frontiers pushed westward, new varieties were necessarily developed to suit climatic and soil variations along the way.

In today's vegetable market, early and late growing kinds with smooth or crumpled leaves of green or purple-red enlarge your choice. Solid well-trimmed heads give the best buy, be they globular, conical, or flat. A puckered variety called Savoy is a little pungent for common palates, but so beautiful as one of nature's plant patterns, it's used as decoration. Avoid the soft, puffy head, or the head with yellow or withered leaves, telltale signs of "old" cabbage.

To prevent wilting, sprinkle cabbage with water, then wrap in clear plastic wrap or foil for storage in the vegetable crisper. Use early spring cabbages immediately for greatest succulence. Late season heads store better than the early, are likely firmer, but none the less choice.

COPENHAGEN CABBAGE

6 cups shredded cabbage
1 cup dairy sour cream
½ teaspoon caraway seed
Salt and pepper

Cook cabbage, covered, in a small amount of boiling salted water, just till tender, about 4 to 5 minutes. Drain thoroughly. Combine sour cream and caraway seed. Pour over cabbage and toss lightly. Season to taste with salt and pepper. Place over low heat *just till heated through*. Serves 4.

BEAN-CABBAGE SCRAMBLE

2 slices bacon
1 10-ounce package frozen cut green beans
¼ cup water
2 to 3 tablespoons chopped onion
3 cups coarsely shredded cabbage (about ½ small head)

In a large skillet cook bacon till crisp; remove bacon. Add green beans, water, and onion to skillet; season with salt and pepper to taste. Cover and bring to boiling; simmer 5 minutes. Add cabbage; cover and bring to boiling; simmer 5 to 7 minutes longer. Crumble bacon over top. Serves 4.

PENNSYLVANIA CABBAGE

2 tablespoons salad oil or bacon drippings
4 cups shredded red cabbage (1 medium head)
2 cups cubed unpared apple (2 medium)
¼ cup brown sugar
¼ cup vinegar
¼ cup water
1¼ teaspoons salt
Dash pepper
½ teaspoon caraway seed

Heat oil in skillet; add remaining ingredients. Cover tightly; cook over low heat, stirring occasionally. For crisp cabbage, cook 15 minutes; allow 25 to 30 minutes for the old-fashioned kind. Garnish with raw unpared apple rings. Makes 4 or 5 servings.

VEGETABLE CHOW MEIN

¼ cup butter or margarine
3 cups coarsely shredded cabbage (about ½ small head)
1 cup bias-cut celery slices
1 cup thinly sliced carrot rounds
1 green pepper, cut in strips
½ cup chopped onion
1 teaspoon salt
Dash pepper
1 6-ounce can (⅔ cup) evaporated milk

Melt butter in large skillet; add cabbage, celery, carrots, green pepper, onion, salt, and pepper. Cover and cook over medium heat just till vegetables are slightly tender, about 5 minutes. Add milk; heat thoroughly, stirring gently once or twice. Serves 6.

SUNNY CABBAGE WEDGES

6 cabbage wedges (1 medium head)
3 tablespoons butter or margarine
3 tablespoons all-purpose flour
1½ cups milk
3 tablespoons prepared mustard
½ teaspoon salt

Cook cabbage in boiling salted water until tender, about 12 to 15 minutes. Drain well. Melt butter in saucepan; blend in flour; add milk and cook until thick, stirring constantly. Stir in mustard and salt. Pour hot sauce over cabbage wedges. Serves 6.

EMERALD CABBAGE

2 tablespoons butter or margarine
3 cups shredded cabbage (about ½ small head)
1 cup sliced celery
½ cup sliced green pepper
¼ cup sliced onion
½ teaspoon salt
¼ teaspoon monosodium glutamate
Dash pepper

Melt butter; add cabbage, celery, green pepper, onion, salt, monosodium glutamate, and pepper. Cover and cook vegetables over low heat 10 to 12 minutes, stirring occasionally. Serve at once. Makes 6 servings.

COUNTRY-STYLE CABBAGE

A speedy recipe for a late supper—

1/4 cup butter or margarine
1/2 teaspoon salt
1 medium head cabbage, shredded
1/4 cup light cream
Dash pepper

Combine butter and salt in skillet; heat till butter melts. Add cabbage; cover and cook 5 to 6 minutes, stirring occasionally. Add light cream. Cook 1 to 2 minutes longer or till heated through. Serves 6 to 8.

CABBAGE-CORN MEDLEY

1 small head cabbage, shredded (about 6 cups)
2 cups boiling water
1 teaspoon salt
2 tablespoons butter or margarine
2 tablespoons all-purpose flour
1 cup milk
1 teaspoon salt
1 teaspoon minced onion
1 1-pound can whole kernel corn, drained
2 tablespoons chopped canned pimiento

Cook cabbage, covered, in boiling salted water till tender, about 10 minutes; do not drain. Melt butter in saucepan; blend in flour. Add milk and cook until thick, stirring constantly. Add salt, onion, corn, pimiento, cabbage and cooking liquid. Heat through. Makes 6 to 8 servings.

PAN-FRIED CABBAGE

3 slices bacon
4 cups chopped cabbage
1 tablespoon lemon juice
1/4 teaspoon salt
Dash pepper

Cook bacon until golden brown and crisp; remove bacon. Drain fat and reserve; return 2 tablespoons fat to skillet. Toss cabbage in hot fat until tender, about 10 minutes. Add lemon juice, salt, and pepper. Garnish with bacon. Serves 4 to 6.

SHREDDED CURRY CABBAGE

2 tablespoons butter or margarine
1 medium clove garlic, minced
1 teaspoon curry powder
8 cups coarsely shredded cabbage (about 1 large head)
1 8-ounce can tomato sauce
1/2 teaspoon salt

In a large skillet melt butter; add minced garlic and curry powder and cook for 2 minutes. Stir in cabbage, tomato sauce, and salt. Cover and cook till tender, about 10 minutes, stirring occasionally. Makes 6 to 8 servings.

SAUERKRAUT PROVENCALE

Sour cream makes the tangy difference—

1/3 cup chopped onion
2 tablespoons butter, melted
1/3 cup canned condensed beef broth
1 14-ounce can sauerkraut, drained
2 tablespoons chopped canned pimiento
1/2 cup dairy sour cream
Poppy seed

Cook onion in butter till tender but not brown. Add broth, sauerkraut, and pimiento; mix lightly. Simmer covered for 10 minutes. Serve topped with sour cream and sprinkled with poppy seed. Makes 4 servings.

TOMATO SAUERKRAUT

Try this unusual flavor combination as an accompaniment for beef or pork—

1/2 cup sliced onion
2 tablespoons butter or margarine
1 tablespoon all-purpose flour
1 1-pound 11-ounce can sauerkraut, drained (3 1/2 cups)
1 1/2 cups tomato juice
1 bay leaf, crushed
1/2 teaspoon salt
1/3 cup brown sugar

Cook onion in butter till tender but not brown. Blend in flour. Stir in remaining ingredients. Cover and simmer 30 minutes. Serve hot as a meat accompaniment.

carrots

This attractive yellow or orange-red root vegetable traces back to the parsley family. It is related to dill, anise, and other herbs. In the United States the plant was grown in 1609 in Virginia and soon used by the Indians as food. In Germany carrots were finely chopped and browned and used as a coffee substitute.

Carrots are available fresh throughout the year, and can be used at various stages of maturity. The small tender carrots that are removed when thinning garden rows are delicious; often these young shorties are canned commercially. We've gotten over a notion that the bigger vegetables are necessarily better.

Carrots are marketed in bunches with tops, without tops, or packaged in cellophane bags. If you're buying carrots with tops, don't be tempted if their tops aren't fresh and green. In purchasing good quality carrots, look for those that are firm, clean, fresh in appearance, smooth, well-shaped and of good color. Wilted, flabby, soft or shriveled carrots lack flavor and succulence. The vegetable crisper of your refrigerator will keep carrots fresh and crunchy.

A pleasant complement to most any main dish, carrots star solo, glazed and sauced, or combined with many other vegetables. Versatile carrots brighten up any dinner fare.

A French homemaker dramatizes vegetables and makes them a high light of her meal. A fine example is Carrots Lyonnaise. The julienne strips of carrot are cooked in chicken stock and mingled with butter-tendered onion slices for further cooking.

CARROTS LYONNAISE

1 pound (6 medium) carrots
1 chicken bouillon cube dissolved in ½ cup boiling water
¼ cup butter or margarine
3 medium onions, sliced
1 tablespoon all-purpose flour
¼ teaspoon salt
Dash pepper
¾ cup water

Pare carrots and cut in julienne strips. Cook carrots in bouillon, covered, 10 minutes. Melt butter; add onions and cook, covered 15 minutes, stirring occasionally. Stir in next 4 ingredients; bring to boiling. Add carrots and stock; simmer, uncovered, 10 minutes. Add pinch of sugar. Serves 6.

SUNSHINE CARROTS

5 medium carrots
1 tablespoon sugar
1 teaspoon cornstarch
¼ teaspoon salt
¼ teaspoon ginger
¼ cup orange juice
2 tablespoons butter or margarine

Slice carrots crosswise on the bias—about 1-inch thick. Cook, covered, in boiling salted water till just tender, about 20 minutes; drain. Meanwhile, combine sugar, cornstarch, salt, and ginger in small saucepan. Add orange juice; cook, stirring constantly, till mixture thickens and bubbles. Boil 1 minute. Stir in butter. Pour over hot carrots, tossing to coat evenly. Serves 4.

CARROTS SUPREME

1 tablespoon butter or margarine
1 cup sliced carrots
1 cup bias-sliced celery
½ cup green pepper strips
½ teaspoon salt
Dash pepper
Dash dill weed

Melt butter in heavy skillet; add carrots, celery, and green pepper. Cover and cook over medium heat 7 minutes. Season with salt, pepper, and dill weed. Cook over low heat about 5 minutes longer or till vegetables are just tender. Makes 3 or 4 servings.

GLAZED CARROTS

Mustard adds the special tang! A perfect accompaniment for pork chops—

2 tablespoons butter or margarine
¼ cup brown sugar
2 tablespoons prepared mustard
¼ teaspoon salt
3 cups sliced carrots, cooked and drained
• • •
1 tablespoon snipped parsley

Melt butter in skillet. Stir in brown sugar, mustard, and salt. Add cooked carrots; heat, stirring constantly, till carrots are nicely glazed, about 5 minutes. Sprinkle with snipped parsley. Makes 4 servings.

COMPANY CARROTS

5 cups sliced carrots
1 cup dairy sour cream
1 3-ounce package cream cheese, softened
3 tablespoons minced green pepper
2 tablespoons sliced green onion
½ teaspoon salt
½ teaspoon grated lemon peel

Cook carrots covered in a small amount of boiling salted water till tender, about 8 minutes. Drain well. In saucepan, combine sour cream, cheese, green pepper, green onion, salt, and lemon peel; stir in the cooked carrots. Heat through. Serves 8.

GOLDEN CARROT BAKE

3 cups shredded carrots
2 cups cooked rice
1½ cups shredded process cheese
½ cup milk
2 beaten eggs
2 tablespoons minced onion
1 teaspoon salt
¼ teaspoon pepper
½ cup shredded process cheese

Combine first 5 ingredients; stir in onion, salt, and pepper. Pour mixture into a greased 1½-quart casserole dish. Sprinkle remaining ½ cup cheese atop. Bake in moderate oven (350°) for 50 to 60 minutes. Serves 6.

CANDIED CARROTS

5 medium carrots
¼ cup butter or margarine
¼ cup canned jellied cranberry sauce
2 tablespoons brown sugar
½ teaspoon salt

Slice carrots crosswise on the bias—about ½ inch thick. Cook, covered, in small amount boiling salted water till just tender, about 6 to 10 minutes.

In a skillet, combine remaining ingredients; heat slowly and stir till cranberry sauce melts. Add drained carrots; heat, stirring occasionally, till nicely glazed on all sides, about 5 minutes. Makes 4 servings.

HERBED CARROTS

2 tablespoons butter or margarine
2 tablespoons water
1 teaspoon sugar
4 cups quartered carrots
Salt and white pepper to taste
1 teaspoon snipped parsley
1 teaspoon snipped fresh tarragon *or* ¼ teaspoon dried whole tarragon, crushed

In heavy saucepan combine butter, water, and sugar; add carrots. Cover tightly and cook gently over *low* heat 15 to 20 minutes or till tender. Add remaining ingredients. Serve without draining. Makes 6 servings.

SPICY CARROT STICKS

See how easy it is to add variety to carrots—

2 tablespoons butter or margarine
1 teaspoon cornstarch
½ cup water
. . .
1 teaspoon salt
Dash pepper
4 whole cloves
2 bay leaves
8 medium carrots, cut in thin strips (about 4 cups)

Melt butter and blend in cornstarch. Add water. Cook, stirring constantly, until mixture is thickened. Add seasonings and carrots. Cover pan and simmer 10 to 12 minutes or until carrots are tender. Remove cloves and bay leaves. Makes 6 servings.

PARSLEYED CARROTS

Serve these with an oven meal—

8 medium carrots
½ cup water
2 tablespoons butter or margarine
1 teaspoon sugar
¼ teaspoon salt
Dash pepper
. . .
2 teaspoons snipped parsley

Pare carrots; leave whole and place in a 9x9x2-inch baking dish. Add next 5 ingredients. Cover and bake in a moderate oven (350°) about 1¼ hours. Drain and sprinkle with parsley. Makes 4 to 6 servings.

SKILLET CARROTS

Carrot lovers will cheer and you'll win over new vegetable fans—

8 medium carrots
3 tablespoons butter or margarine
½ teaspoon salt

Coarsely shred the carrots. Melt butter in a skillet and add carrots. Sprinkle with salt. Cover and cook just until tender, about 5 to 8 minutes. Top with snipped parsley.

HONEY-GLAZED CARROTS

Golden carrots are tender and delicious with a glistening butter-honey coating—

10 to 12 small carrots
3 tablespoons butter or margarine
1 tablespoon brown sugar
2 tablespoons honey

Cook carrots in small amount of boiling salted water about 10 minutes or until tender. Drain. In a skillet melt butter; add sugar and honey; simmer mixture for 2 minutes. Add carrots and cook over low heat, turning until well glazed, about 5 minutes. Makes 6 servings.

SWEET-SOUR CARROTS

An interesting new way to prepare an old favorite vegetable—

4 cups carrots, sliced lengthwise
2 tablespoons sugar
2 tablespoons cornstarch
2 tablespoons vinegar
1 cup hot water
Salt and pepper
2 tablespoons butter or margarine

Cook carrots in small amount of boiling salted water about 10 minutes or till tender; drain. Combine sugar and cornstarch; add the next 3 ingredients; cook till thickened, stirring constantly. Add butter and pour over hot carrots. Makes 6 servings.

CARROTS AU GRATIN

3 cups cooked sliced carrots, drained
1 10½-ounce can condensed cream of celery soup
1 cup shredded process cheese
¼ cup fine dry bread crumbs
1 tablespoon melted butter

Combine carrots, soup, and cheese in a 1-quart casserole dish. Combine bread crumbs and butter; sprinkle atop carrot mixture. Bake in a moderate oven (350°) for 20 to 25 minutes or till heated through and crumbs are browned. Makes 4 servings.

cauliflower

In appearance this garden vegetable is very similar to cabbage. Its name came from the Latin term "caulis," meaning stem, stalk, or cabbage and "floris," meaning flower. The thick round head is made up of a tight cluster of flower buds. It is ready for eating before the buds open. The largest leaves encasing the head are pinned together over the head to keep out the sun, thus the head blanches or whitens as it matures. Though it is widely grown in the United States and Western Europe, most of our crop comes from California as it likes a moist climate with warm days and cool nights.

Fresh cauliflower has a bright green jacket surrounding the firm, closely packed creamy white curd. When cooked with care it has a delicate flavor. Too long cooking darkens its color and the flavor is no longer delicate. Head size doesn't affect the quality, nor do the leaves occasionally found growing through the curds. Yellowed, withered leaves are indicative of age, particularly if the curd has a riced appearance and is beginning to break apart and discolor.

Cauliflower should be kept as cool as possible. Store at a temperature between 32 and 40 degrees. Lessen the wilting of the leaves by sprinkling with water. The green outer stalks may be cooked and served as a vegetable. For refrigerator storage, cauliflower may be wrapped in foil or clear plastic wrap.

Cheese, mayonnaise, and mustard combine to make a flavorful no-cook "frosting" for a head of cauliflower. The attractive golden color is a pleasant complement to the tiny white flowerets. Complete the vegetable platter with buttered whole green beans.

FROSTED CAULIFLOWER

1 medium head cauliflower
Salt
½ cup mayonnaise or salad dressing
2 teaspoons prepared mustard
¾ cup shredded sharp process American cheese

Leaving the cauliflower whole, remove leaves and woody base; wash. Cook cauliflower 12 to 15 minutes in boiling salted water to cover; drain well. Place cauliflower in shallow baking pan. Sprinkle with salt. Mix mayonnaise and mustard; spread over cauliflower. Sprinkle with cheese.

Bake in moderate oven (375°) about 10 minutes or till cheese melts. Transfer to warm platter. Makes 4 or 5 servings.

VEGETABLE MEDLEY

Perfect for an electric fry pan—

2 tablespoons salad oil
2 cups small fresh cauliflowerets
2 10-ounce packages frozen peas
½ teaspoon salt
Dash pepper
2 tablespoons chopped canned pimiento

Heat oil in skillet. Add cauliflowerets and cook covered over low heat 10 to 12 minutes, stirring occasionally. Add frozen peas, salt, and pepper; cover and cook 10 minutes longer, separating peas with fork if necessary. Stir in chopped pimiento. Season to taste with salt and pepper. Makes 8 servings.

CAULIFLOWER SCALLOP

1 10½-ounce can condensed cream of celery soup
2 beaten eggs
½ cup shredded sharp Cheddar cheese
½ cup soft bread crumbs
¼ cup snipped parsley
¼ cup chopped canned pimiento
1 tablespoon instant minced onion
½ teaspoon salt
Dash pepper
2 9-ounce packages frozen cauliflower, thawed

Mix together all ingredients. Place in 10x6x1½-inch baking dish. Bake at 375° for 45 minutes or till firm. Serves 6 to 8.

COMPANY CAULIFLOWER

Wash one medium head cauliflower; break into flowerets. Cook covered in small amount boiling salted water till tender, 10 to 15 minutes; drain *well.* Place *half* the flowerets in a 1-quart casserole; season with salt and pepper. Spread with ½ cup dairy sour cream and ½ cup shredded sharp process American cheese. Top with 1 teaspoon toasted sesame seed; repeat layers. Bake at 350° till cheese melts and sour cream is heated through, about 5 minutes. Makes 6 servings.

SUMMER SCRAMBLE

2 tablespoons butter or margarine
½ cup chopped onion
1 small clove garlic, crushed
¼ cup snipped parsley
1 teaspoon salt
1 teaspoon seasoned salt
Dash *each* pepper and thyme
1 medium head cauliflower, broken into small flowerets
3 large tomatoes, diced
2 small zucchini, sliced

In a large saucepan melt butter; cook onion and garlic until tender but not brown. Add remaining ingredients. Cover tightly; simmer 15 to 20 minutes; uncover and cook about 10 minutes longer. Serve in sauce dishes with juice. Makes 10 servings.

TEMPURA

Tempura is a unique Japanese method of cooking vegetables. Small batter-dipped pieces of vegetable are deep-fat fried till light brown, with an almost "sheer" crust, and not a trace of greasiness. The vegetables actually steam-cook when the icy-cold batter hits the hot fat.

The recipe for Tempura Cauliflower is given below. Use the same tempura batter to experiment with other vegetables, such as asparagus, parsley, sliced sweet potatoes, spinach, mushrooms, and green beans. Serve these vegetables with the same tempura condiments listed in the cauliflower recipe.

Tips to insure your success with tempura:

1. Wash vegetables and *dry well.* Cut into slices where necessary.
2. Cover and chill sauces and condiments if prepared ahead of time.
3. Mix batter just before using; keep chilled with ice cubes while using.
4. Use one set of tongs to dip vegetables in batter; another, for frying.
5. Use fresh, bland cooking oil for frying.

TEMPURA CAULIFLOWER

1 large head cauliflower
Tempura Batter
1 cup sifted all-purpose flour
1 cup ice water
1 slightly beaten egg
2 tablespoons salad oil
½ teaspoon *each* sugar and salt
Tempura Condiments
Grated fresh gingerroot
Equal parts grated turnip and radish, combined
1½ tablespoons soy sauce mixed with ¼ cup prepared mustard

Remove cauliflower leaves and some of the woody stem. Separate into flowerets; wash; dry *very* thoroughly on paper towels.

Just before using, beat together flour, water, egg, oil, sugar, and salt till all dry ingredients are just well moistened (a few flour lumps should remain). Keep batter cool with one or two ice cubes in the batter.

Dip flowerets in batter; cook in deep hot fat (360° to 365°) till tender and browned. Skim off any batter on surface of fat. Drain thoroughly. Serve with condiments.

corn

Ask any man to name his favorite vegetables, and corn is likely to be among them. As American as baseball or hamburger, corn has known this continent for centuries. Columbus found it here, not in wild form, but cultivated for food and tobacco.

Today's corn operates in the space-age class, keeping pace with modern eating habits. Barbecuers all over America know the caramel-sweet goodness of hot charcoal-roasted corn. Served with fluffy, seasoned butters, it's a hit at any patio get-together.

Corn-winning ways are abundant enough to suit every occasion. While corn-on-the-cob may top the popularity list, the variety of corn isn't limited to this form. Casseroles, relishes, fritters, scallops, and puddings combine for a grand collection of golden favorites.

Straight rows of plump kernels mark the best in fresh corn. These milky beads age quickly though, so must be used right away for best enjoyment. Husks should be green and fresh looking—any dryness means the ears aren't at their flavor peak. To capture the sweetness of fresh corn, chill it fast in the refrigerator. For areas of our country with blustery winters, freezing allows fresh corn flavor the year round. What a treat to be served a corn dish in December!

CORN ON THE COB

Delectable, legendary, regional corn rushed from garden to kettle—

Remove husks from fresh corn. Remove silks with stiff brush. Rinse corn. Cook covered, in small amount of boiling salted water about 6 to 8 minutes. (Or, if you prefer, cook in enough boiling salted water to cover.) For ease in eating, insert pronged plastic handles in the ears of corn. Serve hot with plenty of butter—plain or whipped. Pass a bowl of chopped chives, shakers of salt and pepper. Good eating anytime!

CORN CURRY

3 tablespoons butter or margarine
1½ to 2 cups cut fresh or frozen corn*
2 tablespoons chopped green pepper
2 tablespoons chopped onion
¼ to ½ teaspoon curry powder
½ cup dairy sour cream
Salt and pepper

Melt butter in skillet. Add vegetables and curry. Cover; cook over low heat till vegetables are just tender, 8 to 10 minutes. Stir in sour cream; season to taste. Heat, stirring constantly. Makes 4 servings.

*Or, use drained canned whole-kernel corn or leftover corn cut off the cob; add to heated vegetables with sour cream.

WESTERN CORN ON THE COB

4 or 5 ears sweet corn

• • •

½ cup soft butter or margarine
1 tablespoon prepared mustard
1 teaspoon prepared horseradish
1 teaspoon salt
Dash freshly ground pepper

Husk corn and strip off the silk. Combine remaining ingredients and cream till light and fluffy. Spread each ear of corn with a little of the butter mixture. Wrap each loosely in foil and bake in a very hot oven (450°) for 20 to 25 minutes. Serve hot.

If desired, sprinkle extra butter with parsley and pass with hot corn.

SQUAW CORN

1 12-ounce can luncheon meat, cut in julienne strips
3 slightly beaten eggs
1 1-pound can (2 cups) golden cream-style corn
¼ teaspoon salt
Dash pepper

Brown meat in a little hot fat. Combine eggs, corn, and seasonings; add to meat. Cook over low heat only till eggs are just set, stirring occasionally. Serves 6.

CREOLE CORN

3 tablespoons chopped onion
3 tablespoons chopped green pepper
2 tablespoons minced fully cooked ham
1 tablespoon fat
1 8-ounce can (1 cup) tomato sauce
½ teaspoon salt
Dash pepper
2 12-ounce cans (3 cups) whole kernel corn

Cook onion, green pepper, and minced ham in fat until onion is golden. Add tomato sauce and seasonings. Heat through. Heat corn and season. Serve sauce over corn. Serves 6.

SCALLOPED CORN AND OYSTERS

¼ cup finely chopped celery
1 can frozen condensed oyster stew, thawed
1 1-pound can (2 cups) cream-style corn
1½ cups medium cracker crumbs
1 cup milk
1 slightly beaten egg
¼ teaspoon salt
Dash freshly ground pepper
2 tablespoons butter, melted
½ cup medium cracker crumbs

Combine first 8 ingredients. Pour into greased 1½-quart casserole. Mix butter with ½ cup cracker crumbs; sprinkle over top. Bake at 350° for 1 hour or till knife inserted halfway to center comes out clean. Serves 6.

CREAMY CORN

Tender corn in satin-smooth sauce—the preparation is only a matter of minutes, a package of cream cheese, and a can of corn—

In a saucepan, combine one 3-ounce package cream cheese, softened, ¼ cup milk, 1 tablespoon butter or margarine, and ½ teaspoon onion salt. Stir over low heat until cheese melts. Drain one 1-pound can (2 cups) whole kernel corn; stir into cheese mixture. Continue to cook until corn is heated through. Garnish with a sprig of parsley or a sprinkle of paprika. Serves 4 or 5.

CRAB 'N CORN BAKE

Melt ¼ cup butter; blend in 2 tablespoons flour. Add ½ cup milk, 1 tablespoon lemon juice, 1 teaspoon prepared mustard, dash pepper, ½ teaspoon *each* prepared horseradish, Worcestershire sauce, monosodium glutamate, and salt. Cook and stir till thick. Add one 6½-ounce can crab meat, flaked, 2 hard-cooked eggs, chopped, one 1-pound can cream-style corn, and one 1-pound can whole kernel corn, drained. Pour into 1½-quart casserole. Top with ½ cup grated Parmesan cheese and ½ cup buttered cracker crumbs. Bake at 350° for 45 minutes. Serves 6.

CORN RELISH

Combine ⅓ cup sugar, 1 tablespoon cornstarch, 1 teaspoon instant minced onion, 1 teaspoon turmeric, ½ teaspoon celery seed, ¼ cup vinegar, ¼ cup water, and one 12-ounce can (1½ cups) vacuum packed kernel corn. Cook and stir till mixture thickens and boils. Stir in 2 tablespoons minced green pepper, and 1 tablespoon minced pimiento. Chill. Makes 1¾ cups.

CORN O'BRIEN

Want to give corn new flavor? Heat it with celery and pimiento—

1 cup diced celery
1/4 cup butter or margarine
1 1-pound 1-ounce can (2 cups) whole kernel corn, drained
1/4 cup chopped canned pimiento
3/4 teaspoon salt
Dash pepper

In a saucepan, combine celery and butter. Cook for 5 minutes; add drained corn, pimiento, salt, and pepper. Cover and cook 10 minutes longer stirring occasionally with a fork. Serve at once. Makes 6 to 8 servings.

CORN AND POTATO SCALLOP

1 1-pound 1-ounce can (2 cups) whole kernel corn, drained
1 10 1/4-ounce can frozen cream of potato soup, thawed
1/4 teaspoon salt
Dash pepper
2 tablespoons butter or margarine
1/4 cup shredded Parmesan cheese

Combine corn, soup, salt, and pepper. Turn into a greased 1-quart casserole. Dot with butter or margarine; sprinkle shredded cheese over top. Bake in a slow oven (325°) for 25 minutes or until heated through. Makes 4 to 6 servings.

FRIED CORN AND ONIONS

Canned Mexican-style corn boasts red and green sweet-pepper bits—

3 tablespoons butter or margarine
1 large mild white onion, sliced
Salt
1 12-ounce can Mexican-style whole kernel corn

Melt butter in skillet. Add onion; sprinkle with salt. Cover and cook over low heat 4 to 5 minutes, shaking skillet occasionally. Add corn; mix. Heat uncovered 3 to 4 minutes longer or till bubbling. Season with salt to taste. Makes about 4 servings.

QUICK CORN PUDDING

Combine one 1-pound 1-ounce can cream-style corn, and one 10 1/2-ounce can cream of chicken soup; stir into 3 well beaten eggs. Add 1 tablespoon instant minced onion, and dash pepper. Pour into a 1 1/2-quart casserole. Place in a pan with 1 inch of water. Bake at 325° for about 1 hour and 15 minutes, or till knife inserted between center and edge comes out clean. Serves 6.

FIESTA CORN BAKE

1 1-pound can (2 cups) golden cream-style corn
1 cup cooked diced carrots
1/4 cup chopped ripe olives
1/4 cup chopped canned pimiento
1/4 cup chopped onion
2 beaten eggs
1 teaspoon salt
Dash pepper
Dash bottled hot pepper sauce
1/4 cup crushed corn flakes

Combine corn, carrots, olives, pimiento, and onion. Add eggs and seasonings. Pour into greased 10x6x1 1/2-inch baking dish. Sprinkle with crushed corn flakes.

Bake in moderate oven (350°) for 30 to 35 minutes. Makes 6 to 8 servings.

TEXAS HOMINY

In a saucepan, blend one 11-ounce can Cheddar cheese soup, 2 teaspoons dried parsley flakes, 1 tablespoon prepared mustard, and dash chili powder. Stir in two 1-pound cans hominy, drained, and 1/4 cup canned pimiento, diced. Heat to boiling. Makes about 4 servings.

SPEEDY CORN FRITTERS

Combine 1 cup buttermilk pancake mix and 1/2 teaspoon baking powder. Add one 8 3/4-ounce can whole kernel corn, drained, and one 6-ounce can evaporated milk. Stir just till blended. Drop by tablespoons into deep hot fat (375°) and cook till golden brown (about 2 minutes). Drain on paper towels. Serve with butter. Makes about 32.

CORN FRITTERS

Remove the husks and silks from 6 ears of fresh corn; rinse. Cut off just the tips of kernels holding knife at an easy angle as shown at left, then scrape the cob. Drain uncooked cut corn, reserving liquid; add enough milk to liquid to measure 1 cup. Sift together 1½ cups sifted all-purpose flour, 2 teaspoons baking powder, and ¾ teaspoon salt. Combine 1 beaten egg with the milk mixture and fresh corn; add to dry ingredients. Mix just till flour is moistened. Drop batter from tablespoon into deep, hot fat (375°). Fry until golden brown, about 3 minutes. Drain fritters on paper towels. Serve with warm maple-flavored syrup or honey. Makes 18 fritters.

CREAMED CORN

Cut kernels from 5 ears fresh corn (about 1½ cups), then scrape cobs. In a skillet, place 2 tablespoons butter or margarine, fresh cut corn, ½ cup light cream, 1 tablespoon sugar, ½ teaspon salt, and a dash pepper. Cover; let simmer for 6 to 10 minutes, stirring occasionally. Serves 4.

HOMINY IN SOUR CREAM

2 tablespoons butter or margarine
2 1-pound 4-ounce cans (5 cups) golden hominy, drained
1 cup dairy sour cream
½ teaspoon salt
Dash pepper

Melt butter or margarine in a heavy skillet. Add drained hominy and sour cream. Season with salt and pepper. Heat through, stirring mixture frequently. Makes 10 servings.

CORN AND TOMATO ESCALLOP

5 ears corn

• • •

3 large tomatoes, peeled and sliced
2 tablespoons finely chopped green pepper
2 teaspoons sugar
Dash salt
¾ cup fine dry bread crumbs
1 tablespoon butter, melted

Husk corn and remove silks; rinse. Split grains of corn and cut from cob. Place *half* the tomatoes and *half* the green pepper in a 9x9x2-inch baking dish; sprinkle with salt and 1 *teaspoon* of the sugar. Add freshly cut corn and sprinkle with salt and remaining 1 *teaspoon* sugar. Add remaining sliced tomatoes and chopped green pepper.

Combine bread crumbs and butter and sprinkle over top. Bake in a moderate oven (350°) for 45 minutes. Makes 6 to 8 servings.

eggplant

The eggplant, originally a tropical perennial found by early explorers in South America, is now grown widely in the United States and Europe. Eggfruit, aubergene, and guinea squash are other names for eggplant, at one time believed to be poisonous. Few plants are as fussy about soil, moisture, and temperature. The pendant purple flowers and woolly green leaves of the plant decorate many gardens and patios in the Near East.

When buying purple eggplant, look for a clear, dark glossy color. Heaviness and firmness of flesh indicate quality. Beware of the dull-skinned fruit—this signals an overripeness and toughness. Although sizes and shapes of eggplant vary, choose pear-shaped fruits from three to six inches in diameter.

Attractive little white eggplants resembling elongated puff balls are common in Europe. Although cooked as you cook the purple variety, they have a more delicate flavor. In the United States these white fruits are often sold as ornamentals.

BLACKBERRY CREEK FARM EGGPLANT

Savory, herb-freshened goodness—

1 medium eggplant
3 leaves fresh marjoram *or* 1/4 teaspoon dried whole marjoram
1/4 cup chopped onion
2 tablespoons butter or margarine
1/3 cup snipped parsley
1/4 cup butter or margarine, melted
1 cup soft bread crumbs
1/4 cup light cream
1/4 cup grated Parmesan cheese

Slice eggplant; pare, then dice (about 4 1/2 cups diced). Add eggplant to small amount boiling salted water to which you have added the marjoram; cook covered 8 to 10 minutes. Drain well. Cook onion in the 2 tablespoons butter till tender but not brown; add to eggplant along with parsley.

Combine melted butter and crumbs. In a greased 8-inch pie plate, arrange a layer of eggplant mixture, then a layer of crumbs; repeat. Pour cream over top; sprinkle with cheese. Bake in moderate oven (375°) for 25 to 30 minutes or until browned. Serves 4.

BAKED EGGPLANT

1 medium eggplant
1/2 cup salad oil
1 clove garlic, crushed
2 tablespoons snipped parsley
Crushed oregano
Salt
Freshly ground pepper
2 medium tomatoes, cut in 1/2-inch slices
Grated Parmesan cheese

Cut eggplant in half lengthwise and place in greased shallow baking dish. Combine oil and garlic; brush *half* over cut surfaces; sprinkle with parsley and oregano. Season with salt and pepper to taste. Top eggplant with tomato slices; drizzle with remaining oil mixture; sprinkle with oregano, salt, and pepper.

Bake uncovered in hot oven (400°) for 45 minutes to 1 hour or till eggplant is tender. Sprinkle with additional snipped parsley before serving. Pass bowl of grated Parmesan cheese. Makes 6 servings.

ROMAN EGGPLANT

Simplest dish Simon ever made—

1 medium eggplant, pared and cut in 1/2-inch slices
1/2 cup butter or margarine, melted
3/4 cup fine dry bread crumbs
1/4 teaspoon salt

• • •

1 8- or 10 3/4-ounce can (about 1 cup) spaghetti sauce with mushrooms
1 tablespoon crushed oregano leaves
1 cup shredded sharp process American cheese or Mozzarella cheese

Dip eggplant in butter, then in mixture of bread crumbs and salt. Place on greased baking sheet. Spoon sauce atop each slice; sprinkle with oregano and cheese. Bake in hot oven (450°) for 10 to 12 minutes or till done. Makes 4 or 5 servings.

SCALLOPED EGGPLANT

Crunchy cheese topping makes this a tasty treat for an oven meal—

1 large eggplant, diced (4 cups)

• • •

1/3 cup milk
1 10 1/2-ounce can condensed cream of mushroom soup
1 slightly beaten egg
1/2 cup chopped onion
3/4 cup packaged herb-seasoned stuffing

• •

1 recipe Cheese Topper

Cook diced eggplant in boiling salted water till tender, 6 to 7 minutes; drain. Meanwhile, gradually stir milk into soup; blend in egg. Add drained eggplant, onion, and stuffing; toss lightly to mix. Turn into greased 10x6x 1 1/2-inch baking dish.

For *Cheese Topper*, finely crush 1/2 cup packaged herb-seasoned stuffing; toss with 2 tablespoons melted butter or margarine; sprinkle over casserole. Top with 1 cup shredded sharp process American cheese. Bake in moderate oven (350°) for 20 minutes or till hot. Makes 6 to 8 servings.

PAN FRIED EGGPLANT

Crusty half-moons please the palate—

Pare 1 medium eggplant. Cut in half lengthwise, then cut crosswise making ½-inch thick slices. Combine 1 slightly beaten egg and 1 tablespoon cold water. Dip eggplant in egg mixture, then in mixture of ½ cup fine dry bread crumbs, ½ teaspoon salt, and dash pepper. Cook in hot oil for 2 to 3 minutes on each side, or till tender and brown. Drain on paper towels. Sprinkle with salt. Keep warm in slow oven while cooking remaining eggplant. Serves 4 to 6.

CHIPPER EGGPLANT

6 or 8 ½-inch slices eggplant, pared
3 or 4 slices sharp process American cheese

• • •

1 slightly beaten egg
¼ cup milk
Dash salt
1 cup crushed potato chips

Cook eggplant covered in small amount boiling water 2 to 3 minutes. Drain well. Place a slice of cheese between 2 slices of eggplant. Combine egg, milk, and salt. Dip both sides of eggplant "sandwiches" in egg mixture; then in potato chip crumbs. Cook in hot salad oil till golden brown, about 4 to 5 minutes per side. Makes 3 or 4 servings.

MEXICAN EGGPLANT

Cook 1 pound lean ground beef and ¼ cup chopped onion in small amount hot fat till meat is browned. Spoon off excess fat. Sprinkle 1 tablespoon all-purpose flour over meat; toss. Stir in one 8-ounce can (1 cup) tomato sauce, ¼ cup chopped green pepper, 1 teaspoon oregano, ½ to 1 teaspoon chili powder, and ½ teaspoon salt.

Slice 1 small eggplant in ½-inch slices (pared or unpared). Season eggplant with salt and pepper; arrange slices over meat. Cover and simmer till eggplant is tender, 10 to 15 minutes. Top with 1 cup shredded sharp process American cheese. Pass grated Parmesan cheese. Makes 4 servings.

BAKED STUFFED EGGPLANT

1 large eggplant
¾ pound ground beef
¼ cup butter or margarine
¾ cup chopped onion
½ cup chopped green pepper
1 8-ounce can (1 cup) tomato sauce
2 teaspoons quick-cooking tapioca
1 teaspoon salt
Dash pepper
¾ cup corn flakes
¼ cup butter or margarine, melted
Grated Parmesan cheese

Cut eggplant in half lengthwise and remove pulp to within ½-inch of skin. Chop pulp coarsely. Lightly brown beef in ¼ cup butter, stirring occasionally. Add onion, green pepper, and chopped pulp; cook 5 minutes. Add ½ *cup* tomato sauce, tapioca, and seasonings. Spoon hot mixture into eggplant shells. Pour remaining tomato sauce atop.

Place in shallow baking dish. Bake in moderate oven (375°) for 30 minutes or till almost done. Mix corn flakes with ¼ cup melted butter and sprinkle atop eggplant. Bake 10 minutes longer, or till topping is lightly browned. Sprinkle with grated Parmesan cheese. Makes 6 servings.

EGGPLANT RATATOUILLE

2 medium onions, sliced (1½ cups)
1 clove garlic, minced
3 tablespoons olive oil
2 small zucchini, cut in ½-inch slices
2 tomatoes, peeled and diced
1 small eggplant, chopped
1 large green pepper, chopped
1 bay leaf
2 teaspoons salt
Dash pepper
3 slices bacon

In Dutch oven cook onion and garlic in hot oil till tender but not brown. Add zucchini, tomatoes, eggplant, green pepper, bay leaf, salt, and pepper. Bring to boil; cover and simmer 30 minutes, stirring occasionally.

Fry bacon till crisp; drain and crumble. Add to vegetables and simmer, uncovered, 10 minutes. Remove bay leaf. Serves 6.

JACKSTRAW EGGPLANT

As with French-fried potatoes, you can't stop eating them—

Cut 1 medium eggplant in half lengthwise; pare. Slice ½-inch thick. Cut slices in ½-inch strips; dip in *Batter*. Drain well on wire rack. Fry in deep hot fat (375°) for 2 to 5 minutes.* Drain on paper towels. Sprinkle with salt. Serve hot. Pass grated Parmesan cheese. Serves 6.

Batter: Mix 1 cup sifted all-purpose flour with ½ teaspoon salt. Combine 1 slightly beaten egg, 1 cup milk, and 1 tablespoon salad oil; add gradually to flour mixture. Beat till smooth.

*Or in shallow hot fat (½-inch deep) 2 to 5 minutes, turning once.

CHEESE BROILED EGGPLANT

1 small eggplant
2 tablespoons salad oil
Mozzarella cheese slices

Cut eggplant into crosswise slices ¼-inch thick; pare. Place on broiler pan. Brush with salad oil; season to taste. Broil till light brown, about 5 minutes; turn; brush and season. Broil for 3 minutes. Top each piece with a cheese slice; broil till cheese melts, about 2 minutes. Serves 4 to 6.

EGGPLANT-TOMATO STACKS

Slice 1 large eggplant in twelve ½-inch slices; pare and sprinkle with salt. Combine 1 beaten egg and 1 tablespoon milk; dip eggplant slices in mixture; roll in fine cracker crumbs; fry in melted butter. Cut 6 slices process American cheese in half.

Arrange half of the eggplant slices on a baking sheet. Top each with a thick slice of peeled tomato and cover with a half slice of cheese; hold together with a toothpick. Add another eggplant slice to each stack and cover with remaining cheese. Bake in moderate oven (350°) till cheese melts, about 10 to 15 minutes. Makes 6 servings.

PICK-A-DILLY EGGPLANT

Sparked-up with a touch of dill—

1 medium eggplant, pared and diced (about 8 cups)
¼ cup butter or margarine
½ cup chopped onion
½ cup chopped celery
¼ cup all-purpose flour
1 tablespoon dill seed
¼ teaspoon salt
2 cups milk
1 cup shredded sharp process American cheese
1 cup fine cracker crumbs
2 tablespoons butter or margarine, melted

Cook eggplant covered in boiling salted water about 5 to 7 minutes; drain. Melt butter in saucepan; cook onion and celery until tender but not brown. Blend in flour, dill seed and salt. Add milk all at once. Cook, stirring constantly, till mixture thickens and bubbles. Stir in shredded cheese. Gently "fold" in cooked eggplant.

Place in 11x7x1½-inch baking dish. Combine cracker crumbs and melted butter; sprinkle over top of casserole. Bake in moderate oven (350°) for 35 minutes. Serves 6.

mushrooms

Romans thought of mushrooms as food for the gods and denied them even to themselves except on festive days and banquets of state. In the courts of France, the castles of Britain, this delicacy was for royalty and rich. In America, mushrooms remained a luxury for those who could afford to dine lavishly.

Mushroom growing began in the States about the time of the Civil War, from imported spawn in Long Island, New York. Today, mushrooms are grown commercially in a number of different ways and in a variety of environments—in abandoned mines, limestone caves, sheltered quarries, or even in cellars.

Cultivated mushrooms have a place in the average diet on the basis of flavor alone. Steaks and mushrooms are almost inseparable companions, but their excellent flavor plays a part in increasing the palatability of other foods too. Those who know the arduousness of their culture don't complain about the price, which is perhaps high enough to continue to call mushrooms "food for the gods."

MUSHROOM TIPS

Buying: Fresh mushrooms should feel dry and firm. Small brown spots or opened caps indicate mushrooms are merely more mature but retain delicate flavor.

Canned mushrooms are available in various can sizes and forms: buttons, whole caps, sliced, stems and pieces, and chopped. Dehydrated and frozen mushrooms are also available commercially.

Storage: To store fresh mushrooms, place on a shallow tray or rack. Lay a dampened paper towel over mushrooms; remoisten towel daily. Place in refrigerator so that cold air will pass freely around mushrooms.

To store cooked mushrooms, place in a covered dish in the refrigerator. (A little lemon juice added to the mushrooms when cooking will retain color during storage.)

Canned and dehydrated mushrooms may be stored on the shelf without refrigeration. Frozen mushrooms should be kept frozen until ready for use.

Preparation: Wipe fresh mushrooms with a damp soft paper towel and snip off the end of the stem. Do not peel. This removes much of the flavor and velvety quality.

To wash fresh mushrooms, be sure only a light stream of cold water runs over them; wipe dry immediately. Do not soak mushrooms. Sprinkle with lemon juice to prevent mushrooms from turning dark.

To prepare dehydrated mushrooms: Place in a bowl (not metal); cover with hot water; place tight fitting lid on bowl; stand in a warm place 20 minutes. Drain well. Place in covered bowl 15 minutes longer to allow the mushrooms to plump up.

Frozen mushrooms should be prepared according to package directions. Canned mushrooms require no preparation.

Use: When browning mushrooms in butter, be sure they are not damp. Dry thoroughly on paper towels. This will allow the mushrooms to brown rather than steam cook. It will also prevent shriveling and loss of juices. They shouldn't be stacked nor should they touch each other while browning.

Best quality raw fresh mushrooms are delicious thinly sliced and tossed in salads or used as a vegetable garnish.

If just the mushrooms caps are needed, keep the stems for later use in sauces, soups, or casseroles. Save the liquid from canned mushrooms to add flavor to sauces and soups.

BOUILLON MUSHROOMS

1/2 cup chopped onion
1/4 cup butter or margarine
2 pints fresh mushrooms, sliced
1 tablespoon all-purpose flour
3/4 cup water
1 chicken bouillon cube
1/4 teaspoon salt
1/4 teaspoon basil, crushed
Dash bottled hot pepper sauce

Cook onion in butter till tender but not brown. Add mushrooms and flour; toss to coat. Stir in water, bouillon cube, salt, basil, and hot pepper sauce. Cook, stirring constantly, until mixture boils. Simmer 8 to 10 minutes, stirring occasionally. Serve piping hot. Makes 4 to 6 servings.

FRESH MUSHROOM SAUTE

1 pint (about 1/2 pound) mushrooms
3 tablespoons butter or margarine
2 teaspoons all-purpose flour
Salt and pepper

Slice mushrooms through cap and stem. Melt butter in skillet; add mushrooms; sprinkle with flour, and mix. Cover and cook over low heat till tender, about 8 to 10 minutes, turning occasionally. Season to taste. Makes 4 servings as broiled-steak accompaniment or 2 servings as vegetable.

Note: For lighter brown mushrooms, omit flour. Cook in 2 tablespoons butter; season.

MUSHROOMS MING TOY

Seasoned with a subtle touch of soy—

1 pint fresh mushrooms
1 tablespoon all-purpose flour
3 tablespoons butter or margarine
1/2 teaspoon soy sauce
Dash *each* salt and pepper

Wash the mushrooms in small amount of water; don't soak or peel. Cut off tip of stem. Leave mushrooms whole, or slice. Sprinkle lightly with flour. Cook, covered in butter and soy sauce over low heat till tender, about 8 to 10 minutes, turning occasionally. Season. Makes 4 servings.

DILL-HERBED MUSHROOMS

Dill imparts delightful freshness—

1 pint (about 1/2 pound) mushrooms
2 tablespoons butter or margarine

• • •

1 cup dairy sour cream
1 teaspoon dill seed
1/4 teaspoon salt
Dash freshly ground pepper
Dash nutmeg
Hot toast points

Slice larger mushrooms through cap and stem. Melt butter in skillet; add mushrooms and cover. Cook, stirring occasionally, over medium heat about 8 minutes or till lightly browned. Stir in sour cream and seasonings. Reduce heat; cook and stir over low heat just till heated through. Dash with paprika. Serve over toast points. Serves 3 or 4.

Note: You can use one 6-ounce can (1 1/3 cups) broiled sliced mushrooms. Melt butter or margarine; add drained mushrooms; cook about 3 minutes. Stir in dairy sour cream and seasonings; continue recipe as above.

CREAMED MUSHROOMS

Perfectly splendid with broiled steak or for a fancy luncheon main dish—

1 pint (about 1/2 pound) mushrooms
3 tablespoons butter or margarine
1 tablespoon all-purpose flour

• • •

1 teaspoon soy sauce
3/4 cup light cream
Salt and pepper to taste

Slice mushrooms through cap and stem. Melt butter in skillet; add mushrooms. Sprinkle flour over mushrooms; toss to coat. Cook, stirring occasionally, over medium heat about 8 to 10 minutes or till tender and lightly browned. Add soy sauce; slowly stir in cream. Cook and stir till mixture bubbles and thickens. Season. Serve with broiled steak or spoon over hot toast points. Serves 4.

Note: You can use one 6-ounce can (1 1/3 cups) broiled sliced mushrooms. Melt 2 tablespoons butter or margarine; add drained mushrooms; sprinkle with flour; cook 3 minutes. Add soy sauce; continue as above.

BUFFET MORNAY

Arrange two 6-ounce cans broiled mushroom crowns, drained, hollow side up in 8-inch baking dish. Cover with one 6 1/2- to 7 3/4-ounce can crab meat, flaked; sprinkle with 2 teaspoons lemon juice. Melt 3 tablespoons butter; blend in 3 tablespoons all-purpose flour. Add 1 1/2 cups milk all at once; cook and stir till thickened. Add small amount hot mixture to 2 slightly beaten egg yolks; return to sauce; cook 1 minute. Remove from heat; stir in 1 1/4 cups shredded process cheese and 2 tablespoons sherry; pour over crab. Sprinkle with 1/4 cup shredded cheese. Bake at 350° for 20 minutes or till hot. Serve over rice or toast. Serves 6.

MUSHROOMS ELEGANTE

Bubbling with rich, creamy goodness—

1 pint fresh whole mushrooms
3 tablespoons butter or margarine
2 tablespoons minced onion
1 tablespoon all-purpose flour
Dash *each* salt and pepper
1 cup light cream
2 tablespoons grated Parmesan cheese
1 tablespoon lemon juice
2 slightly beaten egg yolks

• • •

1 teaspoon butter, melted
1 tablespoon dry bread crumbs

Wash and clean mushrooms; slice thin. Melt 3 tablespoons butter in skillet; add mushrooms and onion. Sprinkle with flour and toss to coat. Season with salt and pepper. Cook over low heat till tender, about 15 minutes. Stir in cream, Parmesan cheese, and lemon juice; heat through.

Add small amount of hot cream mixture to egg yolks; mix and return to cream mixture. Cook and stir 1 minute longer. Serve in sauce dishes. Garnish with 1 teaspoon melted butter mixed with crumbs. Serves 6.

STUFFED MUSHROOMS

Serve these smoky-flavored appetizers sizzling hot to hungry guests—

2 6-ounce cans (2⅔ cups) broiled mushrooms crowns*
1 tablespoon finely chopped onion
1 teaspoon salad oil
¼ cup finely chopped salami
¼ cup smoke-flavored cheese spread
1 tablespoon catsup
Fine soft bread crumbs

Drain mushrooms. Hollow out crowns and chop enough pieces to make 3 tablespoons; cook pieces with onion in oil. Stir in next 3 ingredients. Stuff into mushroom crowns; sprinkle with crumbs. Bake on baking sheet at 425° for 6 to 8 minutes or till hot.

*Or use 2 pints fresh mushrooms. Wash; trim off tips of stems. Remove stems and chop enough pieces to make ⅓ cup. Continue recipe as above.

MUSHROOMS AND WILD RICE

1 6-ounce can (1⅓ cups) broiled sliced mushrooms
1 can condensed beef broth
2 medium onions, finely chopped
½ cup wild rice, washed
1 cup long-grain rice
2 tablespoons butter or margarine
2 tablespoons snipped parsley

Drain mushrooms, reserving liquid. Combine mushroom liquid and beef broth; add water to make 2 cups. In saucepan bring broth mixture and onions to boiling. Add washed wild rice; reduce heat, cover and simmer 20 minutes. Add long-grain rice; return to boiling; cover and simmer 20 minutes longer. Add mushrooms and butter; heat through; add parsley. Makes 6 to 8 servings.

SHERRIED MUSHROOMS

Wash and slice 1 pint fresh mushrooms. Melt 2 tablespoons butter or margarine in skillet; add mushrooms and 1 tablespoon flour; toss to coat. Add one 8-ounce can tiny white onions, drained, 1 tablespoon snipped parsley, 1 bay leaf, dash nutmeg, and 1 chicken bouillon cube dissolved in ¼ cup boiling water. Cook covered over low heat, stirring occasionally, 6 to 8 minutes or till mushrooms are tender. Add 2 tablespoons sherry; remove bay leaf. Serves 4.

BLUE-CHEESED MUSHROOMS

12 to 14 large fresh or canned whole mushrooms
¼ cup chopped green onions
¼ cup butter or margarine
¼ cup (1 ounce) crumbled blue cheese
⅓ cup fine dry bread crumbs

Remove stems from mushrooms; chop stems. Cook stems and onions in butter till tender but not brown. Add cheese, 2 *tablespoons* of the crumbs, and salt and pepper to taste. Fill mushroom crowns with mixture; sprinkle with remaining crumbs. Place on baking sheet. Bake in moderate oven (350°) for 12 minutes for fresh mushrooms or 8 minutes for canned. Makes 4 to 6 servings.

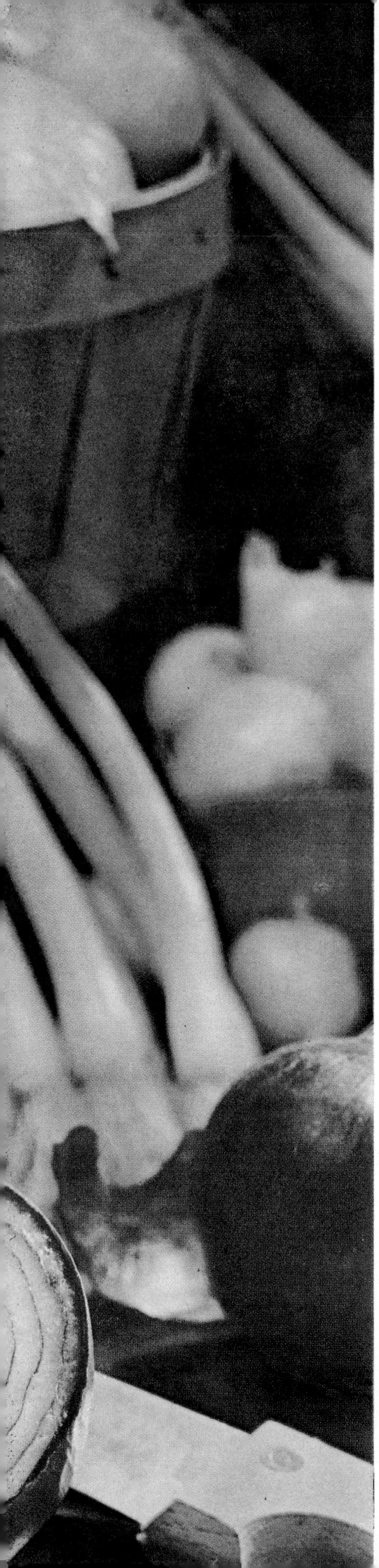

onions

Though we may try to avoid them at times, we could not easily do without onions. Served either as a vegetable or as a zesty flavoring ingredient, their presence makes "all the difference" in many a meat, vegetable, casserole, and salad dish.

Man has used members of the onion family for centuries. The Bible records that the Israelites used onions, leeks, and garlic in Egypt. Indeed the onion was immortalized on Egyptian monuments and used as a symbol of eternity because of its sphere within a sphere formation.

The potency of onions has been favored for other roles too—from a general insurance for good health, to a beauty aid.

Shown here are just a few family members. Vibrant color marks the Red Italian, while its mild-mannered cousin, the Sweet Spanish, wears a subtle brown. In the background are familiar Bermudas—so good with salads and sandwiches. Thin-necked green onions or scallions stand ready for eating without cooking. Small, mild boiling onions are especially popular during holiday seasons when cooked and served whole.

When buying, look for bright-colored, hard onions with clean, dry skins. If a sprout has formed, chances are the onion will be woody. All onions except scallions and leeks fare best when stored in a dry, well-ventilated place.

ONION TIPS

Small white onions can be peeled in a jiffy. Simply cut off tops and roots, cover onions with boiling water, and let stand a minute or two. Then the skins will slip off easily.

If peeling onions makes you cry, try doing this job under cold running water.

To chop an onion without letting it "get away," cut it lengthwise in half from root to stem; peel. Place the flat cut surface down and slice lengthwise several times. Then cut crosswise. One medium onion will make approximately ½ cup chopped.

Fine chopping or mincing is a job for the French chef's knife. Hold handle in right hand. With fingers of left hand, hold point of knife down on cutting board. Using the knife point as a pivot, swing blade up and down, back and forth chopping finely.

Let one cutting job work for you later. Chop or mince a quantity of onion and freeze. Then measure out the teaspoons and tablespoons as you need them.

Always wrap cut onion before storing in the refrigerator. Then the onion odors will not penetrate other foods.

Onion juice is no problem if you draft your lemon squeezer. You'll find "squeezing" an onion twice as fast as grating it. For ¼ cup or more, hold juicer over glass measuring cup for exact amount.

To remove the odor of onions from your hands, rub them with a little lemon juice or vinegar, then wash in soap and water.

APPLE AND ONION BAKE

4 medium onions
3 medium tart apples, pared

• • •

3 tablespoons all-purpose flour
2 tablespoons sugar
1 teaspoon salt
Dash pepper
2 tablespoons butter or margarine

Peel onions; core apples. Thinly slice onions and apples crosswise. Combine flour, sugar, salt, and pepper. Toss apples in flour mixture. Arrange apple and onion slices in alternate layers in a 2-quart casserole. Dot with butter or margarine.

Cover and bake in a moderate oven (350°) for 60 minutes or till tender. Serves 6.

LEEK LORRAINE

1 9-inch unbaked pastry shell
1 1¾-ounce envelope dry cream of leek soup mix
1½ cups milk
½ cup light cream

• • •

3 slightly beaten eggs
1½ cups shredded Swiss cheese
1 teaspoon dry mustard
Dash pepper
1 4½-ounce can deviled ham
2 tablespoons fine dry bread crumbs

Bake pastry shell (have edges crimped high —filling is generous) in very hot oven (450°) for 7 minutes, or just till lightly browned. Remove from oven; reduce oven to 325°.

In a medium saucepan combine soup mix and milk. Cook and stir till mixture boils; cool slightly. Stir in cream. Combine eggs, cheese, mustard, and pepper. Slowly stir in soup mixture. Mix together deviled ham and bread crumbs. Spread on bottom and sides of pie shell. Pour soup mixture over top.

Bake in a slow oven (325°) about 45 to 50 minutes or till knife inserted in center comes out clean. Let stand about 10 minutes before cutting. Makes 6 servings.

FRENCH-FRIED ONIONS

6 medium Bermuda or mild white onions, sliced ¼ inch thick
2 cups milk
3 eggs
All-purpose flour
Salt

Separate onion slices into rings. Combine the milk and eggs; beat thoroughly and pour into shallow pan. Drop onion rings into pan. With your fingers, swish rings around till well coated. Lift onions out; shake over pan to drain. Then drop in pan of flour, a few rings at a time, coating each well. Place in wire French-frying basket (don't fill more than one-fourth full). Shake off excess flour by giving basket a sharp slap.

Fry in deep hot fat (375°), stirring once with fork to separate rings. When onions are golden, drain on paper towels. Just before serving, sprinkle onion rings with salt. Serve hot. Makes 8 servings.

CREOLE ONIONS

8 medium onions, sliced ½-inch thick
2 slices bacon, diced
1 tablespoon minced green pepper
1 small clove garlic, minced
1 8-ounce can tomato sauce
½ cup chopped fully cooked ham
¼ teaspoon salt
Dash pepper
½ cup grated sharp process American cheese

Cook onion rings in boiling salted water for 10 to 12 minutes, or till tender. Drain *well*. Place in a 1½-quart casserole. Fry bacon till crisp; add green pepper and garlic, and cook till tender. Stir in next 4 ingredients. Pour mixture over onions; bake uncovered at 350° for 20 to 25 minutes. Sprinkle with cheese and return to oven to melt cheese. Serves 8.

HASH-STUFFED ONIONS

Cut top slice from big, cooked onions. To remove centers, loosen with tip of knife. Hold onion in both hands and push bottom with your thumbs. (Save center for creaming.) Snip each onion top two or three times to allow room for stuffing. Spoon canned corned-beef hash into the onion shells. Heap generously. Place stuffed onions in baking pan. Spoon 1 cup consomme, or 1 beef bouillon cube dissolved in 1 cup boiling water, over onions. Bake uncovered in moderate oven (350°) for 30 to 40 minutes.

SESAME CASSEROLE

Drain and halve one 1-pound can whole onions. Place, cut side up, in bottom of a 1-quart casserole. Sprinkle 1 cup herb-seasoned croutons over; top with one 1-pound can cut green beans, drained. Prepare one 1-ounce envelope white sauce mix according to package directions, using 1¼ cups milk. Pour sauce over vegetables. Bake covered at 350° for 30 minutes, or till bubbling.

Combine 2 tablespoons butter or margarine, melted, ½ cup herb-seasoned croutons, and 2 tablespoons sesame seed. Sprinkle over casserole. Bake uncovered at 350° for 10 minutes longer. Makes 6 to 8 servings.

TARTE A L'OIGNON (Onion Pie)

9 or 10 slices bacon, cut in 1-inch pieces
5 medium onions, thinly sliced (about 3 cups)
1 tablespoon all-purpose flour
1 teaspoon salt
¼ teaspoon pepper
1 cup light cream
4 slightly beaten eggs
1 9-inch unbaked pastry shell
Dash nutmeg

Cook bacon till crisp; drain on paper towels. Pour fat from skillet, reserving ¼ cup. Cook onions in reserved fat till tender but not brown, stirring occasionally. Stir in flour, salt, and pepper. Add cream; cook, stirring constantly, till mixture thickens. Remove from heat; add small amount of hot mixture to eggs; return to hot mixture. Pour into pie shell; sprinkle with nutmeg. Bake in a hot oven (400°) about 20 minutes or till knife inserted halfway between outside and center comes out clean. Let stand 5 minutes before serving. Makes 6 servings.

LEEKS WITH LEMON

3 large leeks (1½ pounds)
¼ cup butter or margarine, melted
1 tablespoon lemon juice
¼ teaspoon salt
Dash pepper

Cut green tops from leeks; trim bulb roots and remove 1 or 2 layers of white skin. Wash thoroughly and drain. Cook, covered, in a small amount of boiling salted water till tender, 10 to 15 minutes. Drain thoroughly. Combine remaining ingredients. Pour over leeks and serve. Makes 3 or 4 servings.

DUTCH GLAZED ONIONS

Drain one 1-pound can (2 cups) small whole onions, reserving ¼ cup liquid. In a skillet, combine 2 tablespoons butter, 1 tablespoon sugar, and reserved liquid. Cook and stir till blended. Add onions; cook till mixture browns lightly (about 10 minutes), stirring frequently. Serves 4.

Add unmatched elegance to any dinner occasion with Creamed Onions. Traditionally a favorite with holiday meals, these onions are both an individual and extra delicious vegetable dish with a coat of velvet-smooth cheese sauce studded with crunchy peanuts.

CREAMED ONIONS

18 to 20 medium onions

• • •

1/3 cup salad oil
3 tablespoons all-purpose flour
1 1/2 cups milk
1 cup shredded process American cheese

• • •

Peanuts, chopped

Peel onions and cook in a large amount of boiling salted water until tender; drain. In a large saucepan, blend salad oil and flour; stir in milk and cook slowly until mixture thickens, stirring constantly.

Add the shredded cheese and stir until melted. Add drained onions and heat through. Place in vegetable bowl and sprinkle with chopped peanuts. Makes 6 to 8 servings.

PAPRIKA ONIONS

4 large Bermuda onions
Salt

• • •

1/4 cup honey
1/4 cup vinegar
2 tablespoons salad oil
1 teaspoon dry mustard
1/2 teaspoon salt
1/2 teaspoon paprika

Peel onions; cut in half and place cut sides up in single layer in skillet. Add water to almost cover; salt lightly. Cover and simmer about 10 minutes; drain well.

Combine remaining ingredients; pour over onions and simmer 30 minutes or till tender. Baste occasionally to glaze. Remove onions to warm serving plate. Bring sauce to boil; spoon over onions. Makes 8 servings.

HERBED ONION SLICES

A special with steak or liver—

1/4 cup butter or margarine
1 tablespoon brown sugar
1/2 teaspoon monosodium glutamate
1/2 teaspoon salt
Dash pepper
2 to 3 large mild onions, cut in 1/2-inch slices
1/4 cup finely chopped celery
2 tablespoons finely snipped parsley
1/2 teaspoon crushed oregano

In a large skillet, melt butter; add next 4 ingredients. Place onion slices in a single layer in skillet. Cover and cook slowly for 10 minutes on the first side. Then turn and sprinkle slices with celery, parsley, and oregano. Cook uncovered 10 minutes longer. Serves 6.

CHEESE STUFFED ONIONS

Peel 6 medium onions; cook in boiling salted water till just tender, about 25 minutes; drain and cool. Remove centers; chop 1/2 cup onion centers and combine with 3/4 cup cottage cheese, 2 tablespoons finely chopped green pepper, 6 slices crisp-cooked bacon, crumbled, 1/2 teaspoon garlic salt, and dash salt. Stuff onion shells and place in 1 1/2-quart casserole. Top with 1/2 cup buttered bread crumbs and 6 strips pimiento. Cover and bake at 350° for 20 minutes; uncover and bake 10 minutes longer. Serves 6.

ONIONS WITH MUSHROOM SAUCE

2 1-pound cans (4 cups) small whole onions
1 cup dairy sour cream
1 tablespoon milk
1/2 teaspoon salt
1 3-ounce can (2/3 cup) broiled sliced mushrooms, drained

In a saucepan, heat canned onions; drain. Blend sour cream, milk, and salt. Stir in drained mushrooms. Cook and stir mixture over low heat till heated through; pour over drained onions. If desired, garnish with a fluff of parsley. Makes 8 servings.

CHEESE-SCALLOPED ONIONS

3 medium onions (4 cups), sliced lengthwise
3 tablespoons butter or margarine
3 tablespoons all-purpose flour
1/4 teaspoon salt
1 cup milk
1 cup shredded sharp process American cheese

Cook onions in boiling salted water until nearly tender (about 8 to 10 minutes); drain well. Place drained onions in an ungreased 1-quart casserole. Melt butter in saucepan; blend in flour and salt. Add milk; cook and stir till mixture boils. Stir in cheese. Pour sauce over onions. Bake casserole uncovered in a moderate oven (350°) for about 40 minutes. Makes 4 or 5 servings.

GOURMET ONIONS

One of the best ways with onions we know. And so easy. Remember them the next time you serve roast beef—

3 tablespoons butter or margarine
1/2 teaspoon monosodium glutamate
1/2 teaspoon sugar
1/4 teaspoon salt
1/4 teaspoon pepper
1/4 cup sherry

• • •

10 to 12 small onions, peeled, cooked, and drained
1/4 cup shredded Parmesan cheese

Melt butter in saucepan; stir in monosodium glutamate, sugar, salt, pepper, and sherry. Add onions and heat quickly (about 5 minutes), stirring now and then. Turn into serving dish and sprinkle with cheese. Serves 6.

GLAZED PEARL ONIONS

Peel 3/4 pound small white onions. Place in saucepan with 2 tablespoons butter or margarine, melted, 1/2 cup chicken broth, and 1/2 teaspoon salt. Cover; boil gently for 10 minutes or till onions are tender. Reduce heat, uncover and simmer till liquid is completely reduced and onions are glazed (about 10 to 12 minutes). Makes 4 servings.

peas

Pop open the protective pod of a sweet green pea, and enjoy the delicate flavor of this wonderful vegetable. The French dramatize them—make them the high light of a meal. Treated with a few subtle herbs, cooked with turgid lettuce leaves and the few drops of water clinging to each tiny pea, this vegetable gives forth full-bodied flavor. So much flavor, in fact, that many Europeans make a meal out of them. French cooks give another good pointer for cooking this vegetable—add a pinch of sugar to the water when cooking peas to emphasize their sweet, mellow flavor.

The Orientals too have a way with peas, a different kind of pea than the full pods we know on this continent. Note the flat pods pictured here with just the beginnings of seeds. Called Chinese pea pods, snow peas, or podded sugar peas, they're barely introduced to heat, then whisked to the table while still crunchy.

While fresh peas come in their own de luxe green package, they should be used soon. The longer they're exposed to air after being picked from the vine, the more tenderness and sweetness they lose. Before peas are shelled, a light sprinkling of water or covering of ice helps keep them fresh. However, unshelled, water only causes them to spoil quickly. Until they're cooked, the best place for tender peas is in a tightly covered container in the refrigerator.

Almost no cooking is the secret of the tender crisp goodness of these specialty peas. Snow Peas with Water Chestnuts are delicately flavored with chicken broth and soy sauce. The vegetables are quickly stir-fried to keep them as crisp as can be. Try the Oriental method of cooking fresh vegetables and you'll make it your own!

SNOW PEAS WITH WATER CHESTNUTS

Tender pea pods retain their pretty green color and crisp texture—

½ pound fresh (2 cups) Chinese pea pods* *or* 1 7-ounce package frozen Chinese pea pods, thawed
1 tablespoon salad oil
1 teaspoon soy sauce
1 medium clove garlic, minced

• • •

1 5-ounce can (⅔ cup) bamboo shoots, drained
1 5-ounce can (⅔ cup) water chestnuts, drained and sliced
1 chicken bouillon cube
¼ cup boiling water

• • •

1 teaspoon cornstarch
1 teaspoon cold water

If fresh peas are used, wash and remove tips and strings. In a preheated medium skillet or wok, place salad oil, soy sauce, and minced garlic. (A wok or coolie pan has a round bottom which fits on a cooking ring that holds it level. Or a wok can go directly over a hibachi.) Cook over low heat till garlic has browned; add peas, bamboo shoots, and water chestnuts. Toss and cook over high heat for 1 minute. Dissolve chicken bouillon cube in the ¼ cup boiling water; add to peas. Cover skillet or wok and cook mixture over medium heat for 2 minutes.

Combine cornstarch and 1 teaspoon cold water. Stir into peas. Cook, uncovered, over high heat till sauce thickens, about 1 minute. Makes 4 servings.

*You eat these pods and all. Instead of shelling them, cook similar to green beans. Edible podded peas, also called podded sugar peas in seed catalogs, are a favorite vegetable with many home gardeners.

PEAS AND ALMONDS

1/4 cup chopped green onions and tops
1 tablespoon salad oil
1/2 pound fresh (2 cups) Chinese pea pods* *or* 1 7-ounce package frozen Chinese pea pods, thawed
1 3-ounce can (2/3 cup) broiled sliced mushrooms, drained

• • •

1 chicken bouillon cube
1/4 cup boiling water
1 teaspoon cornstarch
1 teaspoon cold water

• • •

2 tablespoons toasted slivered almonds

Cook onion in oil till tender, but not brown. Add peas and mushrooms; toss and cook over high heat 1 minute. Dissolve bouillon cube in boiling water. Combine cornstarch with 1 teaspoon cold water; stir bouillon and cornstarch mixture into peas. Cook, uncovered, over high heat till mixture thickens. Toss with toasted almonds. Makes 4 servings.

*Do not shell peas; cook similar to green beans. Edible podded peas are also called podded sugar peas in seed catalogs.

PEAS WITH BASIL

One flavor complements another—

1 10-ounce package frozen peas *or* 1 1/2 cups fresh peas
2 tablespoons butter or margarine
1/4 cup sliced green onions and tops
1 tablespoon snipped parsley
1/2 teaspoon sugar
1/2 teaspooon salt
1/4 teaspoon basil, crushed
Dash pepper

Thaw frozen peas quickly by pouring boiling water over to separate; drain. If using fresh peas cook, covered, in a small amount of boiling salted water till barely tender.

Melt butter; add green onions and tops; cook till tender but not brown, about 5 minutes. Stir in peas and remaining ingredients. Cook, covered, about 5 minutes or until tender. Makes 3 or 4 servings.

CREAMED PEAS AND NEW POTATOES

Chive cream cheese makes the sauce fast and flavorful—

1 1/2 pounds (about 15 tiny) new potatoes
1 to 1 1/2 pounds fresh peas (about 1 to 1 1/2 cups shelled)

• • •

1 4-ounce carton chive whipped cream cheese
1/4 cup milk
1/4 teaspoon salt

Scrub potatoes; pare off narrow strip of peel around center of each. Cook in boiling salted water till just done, 15 to 20 minutes; drain. Meanwhile, cook fresh peas in small amount boiling salted water till tender, about 8 to 15 minutes; drain thoroughly.

For sauce, blend whipped cream cheese with milk. Stir in 1/4 teaspoon salt. Heat and stir over low heat till warm. Combine hot potatoes and peas in a serving dish; pour cream-cheese sauce over. Serve immediately. Makes 4 to 6 servings.

LUXE PEAS AND CELERY

A tasty and colorful vegetable combination. Crisp-cooked celery gives an Oriental touch—

2 tablespoons butter or margarine
1/2 cup bias-cut celery slices
1 3-ounce can (2/3 cup) broiled sliced mushrooms, drained
2 tablespoons chopped canned pimiento
2 tablespoons finely chopped onion
1/2 teaspoon salt
1/4 teaspoon savory
Dash freshly ground pepper

• • •

1 1-pound can (2 cups) peas, drained *or* 1 10-ounce-package frozen peas, cooked and drained

Melt butter or margarine in skillet. Add celery, mushrooms, pimiento, onion, salt, savory, and pepper. Cook uncovered, stirring frequently, till celery is crisp-done, about 5 to 7 minutes. Add peas; heat just till hot. Makes 4 servings.

SPRINGTIME PEAS

Shell 2 pounds fresh peas. Cover bottom of 10-inch skillet with 6 moist lettuce leaves (with a few drops water clinging); top with peas and 1/3 cup sliced green onions. Sprinkle with 1/2 teaspoon *each* sugar and salt, and dash pepper. Make herb bouquet by placing 1/4 teaspoon *each* chervil and thyme, and 1 teaspoon snipped parsley on small square cheesecloth; tie corners together; place in skillet. Cover and cook over low heat 10 to 15 minutes or till peas are tender; remove herbs and lettuce. Drain peas; season with salt; dot with butter. Serves 6.

MINTED PEAS WITH LEMON

A flavorful accompaniment to lamb—

1 10-ounce package frozen peas
2 tablespoons butter or margarine
1 tablespoon fresh mint, finely chopped *or* 1/4 teaspoon dried mint
1 teaspoon grated lemon peel

Cook peas according to package directions; drain. Add butter, mint, and lemon peel; toss to coat peas. Heat through. Serves 4.

QUICK CREOLE PEAS

1 10-ounce package frozen peas
1/4 cup chopped onion
1/4 cup chopped green pepper
2 tablespoons butter or margarine
1 8-ounce can (1 cup) tomatoes
1/2 teaspoon salt
Dash pepper
1 tablespoon cornstarch

Cook peas according to package directions; drain. Cook onion and green pepper in butter till tender but not brown.

Reserve 2 tablespoons tomato liquid. Cut tomatoes in pieces and add to cooked onion. Stir in salt, pepper, and the drained peas. Heat mixture to boiling. Combine cornstarch with the reserved tomato liquid and stir into peas. Cook and stir till mixture thickens and boils. Makes 3 or 4 servings.

PEAS ELEGANTE

Onions, mushrooms, and a bit of thyme do big things for peas—

1/3 cup chopped onion
2 tablespoons butter or margarine
1 1-pound can (2 cups) peas, drained
1 3-ounce can (2/3 cup) broiled sliced mushrooms, drained
1 teaspoon sugar
1/2 teaspoon salt
Dash *each* pepper and thyme

Cook onion in butter till tender but not brown; add peas and mushrooms. Stir in sugar, salt, pepper, and thyme. Cover and cook over low heat till hot through. Serves 4.

SMOKY PEAS

3 slices bacon, diced
1/4 cup chopped onion
2 teaspoons all-purpose flour
1 cup light cream
2 cups shelled fresh peas *or* 1 10-ounce package frozen peas, thawed

Fry bacon till crisp; drain. Cook onion in bacon drippings till tender but not brown. Blend in flour and stir in cream. Add peas; cover and cook, stirring occasionally, till peas are tender. (Allow 15 to 20 minutes for fresh peas and 5 to 10 minutes for frozen peas.) Add bacon; season to taste. Serves 4.

SPANISH GREEN PEAS

Melt 2 tablespoons butter or margarine in a saucepan; add ½ teaspoon onion salt, ¼ teaspoon crushed oregano, and a dash freshly ground pepper. Cook seasonings gently for 3 minutes.

Add one 1-pound can (2 cups) peas, drained, 3 tablespoons chopped canned pimiento, and ¼ cup ripe olive slices; toss lightly to mix. Cover and cook over low heat till peas are hot, shaking the pan occasionally. Makes about 4 servings.

MEXICAN CHICK PEAS

¼ cup finely chopped green pepper
⅓ cup finely chopped onion
1 clove garlic, minced
2 slices bacon, cut up
2 15-ounce cans chick peas, undrained*
½ 6-ounce can tomato paste
¼ cup brown sugar
½ teaspoon salt

Combine first 4 ingredients; cook till tender. Stir in remaining ingredients. Pour into 1½-quart casserole. Bake uncovered in a moderate oven (350°) for 1¾ hours. Stir twice during baking and again just before serving. Makes 8 servings.

*Also called garbanzo beans.

PEAS AND CARROTS

2 10-ounce packages frozen mixed peas and carrots
½ cup thinly sliced green onions
2 tablespoons butter or margarine
2 tablespoons all-purpose flour
¾ cup buttermilk
¼ teaspoon salt
Dash pepper
¼ cup mayonnaise or salad dressing

Cook peas and carrots according to package directions. Add onions during last 2 minutes of cooking time. Melt butter in a saucepan; blend in flour. Add milk all at once. Cook quickly, stirring constantly, till mixture thickens. Add salt and pepper. Blend in mayonnaise and heat through. Drain vegetables and add to sauce. Serves 8.

EPICUREAN PEAS

4 slices bacon, chopped
1 tablespoon chopped onion
1 cup fresh mushrooms, sliced *or* 1 3-ounce can broiled sliced mushrooms, drained
2 tablespoons butter or margarine
1 tablespoon all-purpose flour
1 cup light cream
Salt and pepper to taste
1 1-pound can (2 cups) peas, drained *or* 1 10-ounce package frozen peas, cooked and drained

• • •

Timbale cases

In a skillet fry bacon till crisp; remove bacon from pan. Cook onion and fresh mushrooms in bacon fat till tender. Drain any remaining fat. Melt butter or margarine in a saucepan and blend in flour. Add cream all at once. Cook quickly, stirring constantly, until mixture thickens.

Add salt and pepper to taste. Stir in peas and mushrooms. Add cooked bacon and heat through. Spoon hot mixture into timbale cases. If desired, top with additional crumbled bacon. Makes 6 servings.

TIMBALE CASES

These little "dishes" will make ordinary creamed vegetables a feast—

1 cup sifted all-purpose flour
1 tablespoon sugar
¼ teaspoon salt

• • •

1 cup milk
2 well beaten eggs

Sift flour, sugar, and ¼ teaspoon salt together. Add milk to beaten eggs; gradually stir in flour mixture; beat till smooth.

Heat a timbale iron in deep hot fat (375°) for 2 minutes. Drain excess fat from iron; dip into batter to within ¼ inch of top. Return at once to hot fat. Fry until case is crisp and golden brown and will slip from iron. Turn upside down to drain. Reheat iron 1 minute; make next timbale case. Makes about 2 dozen.

Note: If batter slips off, iron is too cold; if it sticks, iron is too hot.)

peppers

In the West Indies, the spice-seeking Columbus expedition discovered a fruit more pungent than the familiar Far Eastern pepper. Convinced these fruits must be related to the precious table condiment, the explorers coined the misnomer, "pepper."

The plump peppers in the picture are known as sweet, bell, or mango peppers depending upon the location of the market. When buying peppers, look for bright, thick-fleshed fruits with firm exteriors. Soft seeds and pale color signify immaturity. In warm temperatures green peppers will eventually turn red as they reach full maturity, but the flavor will not be impaired. To store peppers, wrap well and refrigerate, preferably in the vegetable crisper.

Chile peppers are the long, slender, green and red peppers shown above. These "hot" fruits are growing in popularity due to greater familiarity with Mexican cookery on the American cuisine front. Other members of the versatile pepper family include the pimiento, thick-fleshed, red sweet peppers, harvested from the paprika plant; pungent cayenne pepper and milder paprika, derived from the dried, powdered pods of different small, slender fruits; and tabasco peppers, which form the base for the zesty sauces made famous by America's Southland.

CHILES RELLENOS CON QUESO

3 fresh long green hot peppers or canned green peeled chiles
1 to 1½ cups shredded sharp Cheddar cheese
All-purpose flour
6 egg whites
3 tablespoons all-purpose flour
Dash salt
6 egg yolks

Cut peppers or canned chiles in half crosswise. (To prepare *fresh* peppers, place on broiler pan; broil 4 inches from heat just till skins blister. Cool slightly. Peel and remove stems and seeds.) Stuff each pepper or chile half with cheese; roll in flour. Beat egg whites until stiff, but not dry. Add 3 tablespoons flour and the salt to yolks; beat till thick and lemon colored; fold into whites.

For each Chile Relleno, spoon a mound (about ½ cup) of egg batter into shallow hot fat (375°); spread batter into a circle. As batter begins to set, gently top each mound with a cheese-stuffed pepper. Cover with more batter. Continue cooking till underside is nicely browned. Turn carefully and brown second side; drain on paper towel. Serve at once. Makes 6 servings.

GREEN PEPPERS AND TOMATOES

½ cup thinly sliced onion
2 cloves garlic, minced
1 tablespoon olive oil
2 cups stewed tomatoes or 1 1-pound can tomatoes
2 teaspoons sugar
¾ teaspoon salt
Dash pepper
½ teaspoon basil
4 to 5 large green peppers, cut in strips ½-inch wide (4 cups)
2 tablespoons olive oil

Cook onion and garlic in 1 tablespoon hot oil until tender; add tomatoes and seasonings. Simmer uncovered till sauce is slightly thick, about 20 minutes. Cook pepper in 2 tablespoons oil, turning frequently, till tender but still *crisp*. Lift to serving dish; top with tomato sauce. Serves 6.

GARDEN PEPPER BOATS

A blend of luscious vegetables—

3 medium green peppers
¼ cup chopped onion
2 tablespoons butter or margarine
1 cup canned whole kernel corn or fresh cut corn
1 medium tomato, chopped (¾ cup)
½ cup cooked baby Limas
1 tablespoon butter or margarine melted
½ cup soft bread crumbs

Remove tops and seeds from peppers. Cut in half lengthwise. Cook peppers in boiling salted water 5 minutes; drain. Cook onion in 2 tablespoons melted butter till tender but not brown. Add corn, tomato, and Limas; mix well. Season pepper shells with salt and pepper to taste.

Fill peppers with vegetable mixture. Combine 1 tablespoon melted butter and bread crumbs; sprinkle atop peppers. Place in 10x6x1½-inch baking dish. Bake in moderate oven (350°) for 30 minutes. Serves 6.

INDIAN STUFFED PEPPERS

Stuff sweet red peppers as well as green ones to brighten up your meal—

1 10½-ounce can condensed beef broth
1¼ cups water
1 6-ounce package long-grain and wild-rice mix
6 medium to large green peppers
1 3-ounce can (⅔ cup) broiled chopped mushrooms, drained
½ cup broken pecans, toasted
⅓ cup buttered bread crumbs

Combine first 3 ingredients; cover and cook, stirring often, about 30 minutes or till rice is done. Meanwhile, cut tops off peppers, leaving shoulders on; remove seeds and membranes. Precook pepper cups in boiling salted water about 5 minutes; drain. Stir mushrooms and pecans into cooked rice.

Spoon about ½ cup rice mixture into each pepper cup; place in 10x6x1½-inch baking dish. Sprinkle tops with bread crumbs. Bake at 350° for 25 minutes. Serves 6.

potatoes

One potato, two potato, three potato, four—put variety in your meals with Idahos, russets, tiny new potatoes, sweet potatoes, or yams. Whether you sauce, sprinkle, shred, or fluff them, make all these different potatoes a means for many a new flavor creation.

Potatoes have been world travelers for a long, long time. Originally from South America, they were first seen in Spain on the European continent. Later, England reintroduced them to the New World. At one time, the "luck of the Irish" depended upon the luck of the potato crop they were able to grow each year.

A few years ago, American restaurants began the custom of serving baked potatoes drizzled with butter. Today, they're glorified from coast to coast with sour cream, cheese, bacon, or chives. This compatibility with a number of different flavors has added to the popularity of potatoes at any meal.

Another reason for the universal use of potatoes is their long storage life. Kept in a dry, cool place, flavor and texture hold their own.

By contrast, sweet potatoes are not good keepers and should be used as soon as possible. Though we use them for the same purpose in our diet, sweet potatoes are actually in a completely different family than white potatoes.

BAKED POTATOES

Choose firm smooth white potatoes for baking. (New potatoes are not suited to baking.) For even cooking, select potatoes all of the same size.

Wash and scrub with a vegetable brush. Or, let a plastic-mesh pad double as a vegetable brush. It will clean potatoes in a jiffy —and save your manicure too. Just rinse pad under tap to clean.

When you bake potatoes solo, set your oven at 425° and bake for 40 to 60 minutes. But if you have other foods in the oven that require lower or higher temperatures, just tuck the potatoes in too—they'll bake nicely anywhere between 350° and 450°. At 350°, they'll take 60 to 80 minutes.

When you halve potatoes for baking, you cut time in the oven in half, too. Brush all sides with cooking oil and place cut side down on a baking sheet. After potatoes are done, turn cut side up and spread with butter or margarine; sprinkle with paprika. Return to oven to brown lightly.

For foil-baked potatoes, wrap clean dry potatoes in foil. Bake at 350° for 1½ hours.

When whole potatoes are done, roll them gently under hand to make mealy. Then immediately cut crisscross in top with fork so steam can escape. Press the ends and push to fluff up the insides.

Baked potatoes stay dry and fluffy if you leave the vegetable dish uncovered or use a platter for serving. When bakers are done, serve them immediately.

They're good eating just plain with a pat of butter melting down. But for variety, try them with a luscious new topper. Or, scooped out, seasoned with salt and pepper, and fluffed, then stuffed back in their jackets.

BAKED POTATO TOPPERS

Whip together 1 cup shredded sharp process American cheese and ¼ cup soft butter or margarine. Add ½ cup dairy sour cream and 2 tablespoons chopped green onion, whip till well blended. Makes 1⅓ cups.

Soften one 8-ounce package cream cheese. Add ⅓ cup light cream; beat fluffy. Add 1 tablespoon snipped chives, 1½ teaspoons lemon juice, and ½ teaspoon garlic salt.

Offer crumbled bacon, snipped chives, sour cream, shredded cheese—one or more.

BLUE CHEESE AND BACON POTATOES

3 medium baking potatoes
½ cup milk
3 teaspoons butter or margarine
½ teaspoon salt
Dash pepper
3 tablespoons blue cheese dressing
3 slices bacon, cooked and drained

Scrub potatoes with brush. Rub with fat and puncture skin with a fork. Bake in a hot oven (400°) for 1 hour. Cut slice from top of potatoes. Scoop out insides; mash. Add milk, butter, salt, and pepper; beat till fluffy Pile lightly into shells.

Garnish each potato with a tablespoon blue cheese dressing and crumble a strip of bacon over each. Return to oven 15 minutes to heat. Serve at once. Makes 3 servings.

POTATO AND ONION BAKE

4 medium baking potatoes, pared
¼ cup butter or margarine, softened
2 medium mild onions, sliced
Salt and pepper

Cut each potato in 4 crosswise slices; spread butter between slices and on top; reassemble with onion rounds between potato slices. Sprinkle generously with salt, then with dash pepper. Secure potato and onion slices together with toothpicks or skewers.

Wrap each potato tightly in double thickness of aluminum foil. Bake on baking sheet in moderate oven (375°) for 60 to 65 minutes, or till potatoes are done. Open foil; sprinkle with chopped parsley or return to oven to brown tops. Serves 4.

BUTTER-SCALLOPED POTATOES

1 quart thin-sliced pared potatoes
⅓ cup butter or margarine

In a 10x6x1½-inch baking dish, arrange ⅓ of potatoes. Dot with ⅓ of butter; dash with salt and pepper. Repeat with two more layers. Cover with foil; bake in a hot oven (425°) about 40 minutes. To brown, uncover last 10 minutes of baking. Makes 8 servings.

Slip skins from hot potatoes the easy way without burning fingers. Score raw potatoes around center with point of knife. Cook covered in boiling salted water till done. Spear each potato with fork tines *in the score mark*, and start peeling there.

POTATO DUMPLINGS

Traditional with Sauerbraten—

6 medium potatoes, pared (2 pounds)
2 slightly beaten eggs
3/4 cup all-purpose flour
1/2 cup farina
1/8 teaspoon nutmeg
1/8 teaspoon cinnamon
1/2 teaspoon sugar
1 teaspoon salt

• • •

2 tablespoons minced onion
1 cup fine dry bread crumbs
1/4 cup butter or margarine

Boil potatoes and put through a ricer (about 4½ cups); let cool. Add next 7 ingredients in the order given; beat well. Then roll mixture into balls the size of a golf ball. Drop into plenty of boiling salted water to cover (1 teaspoon salt to 1 quart water).* Let simmer 20 minutes. Brown onion and crumbs in butter. Drain dumplings; spread tops with crumb mixture. Makes 6 servings.

If desired, omit crumb topping and sprinkle hot dumplings with snipped parsley.

*Shape and test one dumpling first in boiling water; if it falls apart, beat a little more flour into remaining mixture.

SPRINGTIME POTATOES

Fresh, new flavor for potatoes. Great for a fried-chicken dinner—

1½ pounds small new potatoes
1/3 cup chopped cucumber
1½ tablespoons chopped green onion
2 tablespoons chopped green pepper
2 tablespoons sliced radishes
1 teaspoon salt
Dash pepper
1/2 cup dairy sour cream

Wash and scrape potatoes; cook till tender in boiling salted water. Drain. Combine remaining ingredients. Heat, but do not boil. Pour sour-cream mixture over hot potatoes. If desired, garnish with parsley. Serve immediately. Makes 4 servings.

POTATOES MARGARET

1 cup dairy sour cream
1/2 cup milk
1 tablespoon instant minced onion
5 cups sliced cooked potatoes (5 or 6 medium potatoes)
Salt and pepper

• • •

1 tablespoon butter or margarine
2 tablespoons fine dry bread crumbs

Combine first 3 ingredients. Place *half* the potatoes in greased 10x6x1½-inch baking dish. Sprinkle generously with salt and pepper. Add *half* the sour-cream mixture. Repeat layers. Melt butter, add crumbs and toss to mix; sprinkle over top. Bake in a moderate oven (350°) for 20 to 25 minutes. Makes 6 servings.

HERB-FRIED POTATOES

Melt 3 tablespoons butter or margarine in a heavy skillet. Add 3 potatoes, pared and cut in 1/8-inch slices (about 3 cups); cover and cook over medium heat for 10 minutes. Turn potatoes carefully. Cook uncovered 10 minutes more, turning occasionally to brown all sides. Last 5 minutes, sprinkle with ½ teaspoon oregano and 2 tablespoons *each* finely chopped celery, parsley, and onion. Salt and pepper to taste. Serves 4.

BUFFET POTATOES

4 medium baking potatoes
1/4 teaspoon salt
Dash pepper
1 tablespoon snipped parsley
3 tablespoons butter or margarine
1/2 cup grated sharp process American cheese
1/2 cup light cream

Pare potatoes and cut lengthwise in strips as for French fries. Place in center of large piece of aluminum foil (use double thickness if not heavy). Shape foil to form baking dish. Toss potatoes with salt, pepper, and snipped parsley. Dot with butter and sprinkle with grated cheese. Pour cream over. Bring edges of foil up to cover potatoes; seal all edges to make a tightly closed package, but don't press.

Place on baking sheet or shallow pan. Bake in hot oven (425°) for 45 minutes, turning once. To serve, place foil-wrapped potatoes in basket or on serving platter; fold back edges of foil. Sprinkle with extra chopped parsley, salt, and pepper. Makes 4 servings.

FLUFFY POTATOES

Packaged instant mashed potatoes (enough for 4 servings)

• • •

1/2 cup light cream
2 tablespoons grated Parmesan cheese
1 teaspoon instant minced onion
1 teaspoon salt
3 egg yolks
3 stiff-beaten egg whites

Prepare potatoes according to package directions. Add cream; heat over low heat till very hot. Add cheese, onion, and salt. Add egg yolks one at a time, beating well with electric mixer or rotary beater after each addition. Fold a little of the hot mixture into stiff-beaten egg whites. Fold into potato mixture. Pour mixture into an ungreased 1 1/2-quart casserole. With tip of spoon, trace a circle through top, 1 inch from edge and about 1 inch deep.

Bake in a moderate oven (375°) for 30 minutes or till mixture does not adhere to knife. Serve at once with butter. Serves 6.

SKILLET-FRIED POTATOES

Hashed Browns: Chill cooked-in-jacket potatoes, peel, shred to make 4 cups. Add 1 to 2 tablespoons grated onion, 1 teaspoon salt, and dash pepper. Melt 1/3 cup butter or drippings in 10-inch skillet. Pat potatoes into pan, leaving *1/2-inch space* around edge.

Brown 10 to 12 minutes; peek. Reduce heat if necessary. Brown 8 to 10 minutes longer, till golden. (If desired, mark through center, loosen, flip one half over other.) Place platter over pan; invert.

Cottage Fries: Cook potatoes in jackets; peel. Slice or dice. Fry in bacon drippings or other fat till brown and crisp, turning frequently. Season with salt and pepper.

Lyonnaise Potatoes: Add thinly sliced onion to Cottage Fries during cooking.

Fresh-fried Potatoes: Pare 3 medium potatoes; slice thin. Season; fry, covered, in 3 tablespoons bacon drippings or other fat 10 minutes. Uncover and brown other side, about 10 minutes, loosening slices occasionally.

DUCHESS POTATOES

2 cups hot mashed potatoes
1 tablespoon butter or margarine
1 beaten egg yolk
Salt
Pepper
1 tablespoon butter or margarine, melted

To mashed potatoes, add 1 tablespoon butter or margarine, the beaten egg yolk, and salt and pepper to taste; mix well. Push mounds of potato mixture from large spoon onto greased baking sheet. Drizzle with 1 tablespoon melted butter or margarine. Bake in a very hot oven (450°) for 10 to 12 minutes. Makes 4 to 6 servings.

COMPANY POTATOES

Prepare 4 servings of instant whipped or mashed potatoes according to package directions. Just before serving, stir in 1/2 cup to 1 cup dairy sour cream and 1 tablespoon chopped canned pimiento; add salt to taste; heat, stirring constantly, just till hot. Snip parsley or chives over top.

DILL POTATOES

Pare $1\frac{1}{2}$ pounds (about 15) tiny new potatoes; cook in boiling salted water till tender, 15 to 20 minutes; drain. Melt 1 tablespoon butter; blend in 2 teaspoons all-purpose flour, $\frac{1}{2}$ teaspoon salt, $\frac{1}{4}$ teaspoon dried dill weed *or* 1 teaspoon snipped fresh dill weed. Add $\frac{1}{3}$ cup milk, and $\frac{3}{4}$ cup light cream all at once. Cook and stir over medium heat till mixture thickens. Reduce heat; add potatoes; heat through. Sprinkle with additional dill weed. Serves 4 or 5.

POTATOES IN LEMON SAUCE

2 pounds potatoes
$\frac{1}{4}$ cup butter or margarine
1 tablespoon lemon juice
1 tablespoon snipped green onion tops
Dash pepper
Dash nutmeg
1 teaspoon grated lemon peel

Pare potatoes; cook in boiling salted water, covered, till done, about 30 minutes. Drain and set aside. In small saucepan, heat butter with next 4 ingredients. Pour over potatoes, coating each potato well. Sprinkle with grated lemon peel. Makes 6 servings.

CHEESE STICKS

1 1-ounce package white sauce mix
$\frac{1}{2}$ teaspoon onion salt
1 cup shredded sharp Cheddar cheese
1 tablespoon chopped canned pimiento
1 16-ounce package frozen French-fried potatoes

Prepare white sauce mix according to package directions. Stir in onion salt, pimiento, and $\frac{1}{2}$ *cup* of the cheese. Place potatoes in $10x6x1\frac{1}{2}$-inch baking dish; top with sauce. Sprinkle remaining cheese on top. Bake at 350° for 25 to 30 minutes. Serves 4.

SCALLOPED POTATOES

2 quarts thin-sliced pared potatoes (about 8 medium)
$\frac{1}{4}$ cup chopped green pepper
$\frac{1}{4}$ cup minced onion
1 $10\frac{1}{2}$-ounce can condensed cream of mushroom soup
1 cup milk
2 teaspoons salt

In greased $11x7x1\frac{1}{2}$-inch baking dish or 2-quart casserole alternate layers of potatoes, green pepper, and onion. Combine remaining ingredients, dash pepper; pour over. Cover; bake at 350° for 45 minutes. Uncover and bake 20 to 30 minutes longer or till potatoes are tender. Serves 8.

FRENCH FRIES

Cut pared baking potatoes lengthwise in strips. Soak 1 hour in cold water. Drain thoroughly between towels. Fry small amount of potatoes at a time in deep, hot fat (360°) until just light brown. Drain on paper towels. Let cool thoroughly. Cover and refrigerate until serving time.

Just before serving, reheat fat to 375°. Then return potatoes for about 3 to 5 minutes, or till crisp and golden brown. Drain on paper towels. Sprinkle with salt and pepper to taste and serve while hot.

Note: Do not French-fry new potatoes.

POTATO PANCAKES

Crispy edged and delicious—

6 medium potatoes, pared (2 pounds)
1 small onion, grated
2 tablespoons all-purpose flour
4 strips crisp-cooked bacon, crumbled
2 beaten eggs
1½ teaspoons salt
Dash pepper
Dash nutmeg
2 tablespoons chopped parsley

• • •

Butter or margarine

Cover potatoes with cold water; drain. Grate at once and drain off water that collects in grating. Mix potatoes, onion, flour, bacon bits, eggs, and seasonings, blending well. Heat butter (enough to be ¼ inch deep) in skillet. Just before butter turns brown, drop in ⅓ cup batter for each pancake, and flatten them out. When golden brown on one side, turn pancakes over and cook until crisp and brown on other side. Remove to paper towels; keep warm while frying remaining pancakes. Makes 6 servings or 12 five-inch cakes.

POTATO-PEA CASSEROLE

1 2¾-ounce envelope dry smoky green pea soup mix
3½ cups milk
Packaged dry hash brown potatoes (enough for 4 servings)
2 tablespoons butter or margarine
1 12-ounce can luncheon meat, cubed
½ cup shredded sharp Cheddar cheese
Dash paprika

In a large saucepan, combine soup mix and milk. Heat and stir till soup boils; reduce heat, cover and simmer 15 to 20 minutes or till peas are tender. Remove from heat, stir in potatoes and butter. Fluff with a fork. Stir in canned luncheon meat.

Turn into a 1½-quart casserole; bake in a moderate oven (350°) for 20 to 25 minutes. Sprinkle shredded cheese over; return to oven till cheese melts. Before serving dash top with paprika. Makes 4 to 6 servings.

DEVILED POTATO PATTIES

6 medium potatoes, cooked and shredded (4 cups)
1 4½-ounce can deviled ham
3 tablespoons finely chopped onion
2 tablespoons all-purpose flour
2 tablespoons snipped parsley
1 tablespoon prepared mustard
½ teaspoon salt

• • •

¼ cup butter or margarine
⅓ to ½ cup evaporated milk *or* **light cream**

Lightly toss together potatoes, deviled ham, chopped onion, flour, snipped parsley, mustard, and salt. Form mixture into 6 patties. Brown one side slowly in butter. Spoon evaporated milk over patties; cook till milk is absorbed and bottoms of patties are crusty. Turn; cook till other side is crusty. Makes 6 servings.

PARSLEYED NEW POTATOES

Scrub or scrape 1½ pounds tiny new potatoes. Cook in boiling salted water till just tender, 15 to 20 minutes; drain. Peel if desired. Meanwhile, melt ¼ cup butter in a saucepan; stir in ¼ cup snipped parsley and 1 tablespoon lemon juice. Pour over hot potatoes. Serves 4 to 6.

PARMESAN POTATO BAKE

Packaged dry hash brown potatoes (enough for 4 servings)
1 10¼-ounce can frozen condensed cream of potato soup
1 soup-can milk
1 tablespoon instant minced onion
1 tablespoon snipped parsley
Dash pepper

• • •

⅓ cup shredded Parmesan cheese

Prepare potatoes according to basic recipe on package. Combine remaining ingredients except cheese. Heat till soup thaws; add to drained potatoes, mixing gently. Turn into 10x6x1½-inch baking dish. Sprinkle with cheese. Bake in moderate oven (350°) for 35 minutes or till top is lightly browned. Top with snipped parsley. Makes 6 servings.

SKILLET POTATOES

4 medium potatoes, pared and cubed (about 4 cups)
½ cup finely chopped onion
1 teaspoon salt
Dash pepper
1½ cups light cream
¼ cup butter or margarine, melted
¾ cup shredded sharp process cheese
½ cup buttered bread crumbs
3 slices crisp-cooked bacon, crumbled

Combine potatoes and next 5 ingredients in heavy skillet; cover and cook over low heat 20 minutes, or till potatoes are tender, stirring once or twice. Stir in cheese. Turn into serving dish and top with crumbs and bacon. Makes 6 servings.

FILLED POTATO NESTS

2 cups prepared instant mashed potatoes
1 slightly beaten egg yolk
1 egg white
½ teaspoon paprika
1 1-pound can (2 cups) mixed vegetables, drained
½ teaspoon onion salt
1 cup shredded sharp process American cheese

Mix mashed potatoes and egg yolk. On greased baking sheet, form into 4 nests. Beat egg white and paprika slightly; brush over potatoes. Mix vegetables and onion salt; spoon into nests. Sprinkle cheese over top. Bake at 400° for 25 to 30 minutes or till lightly browned. Serves 4.

GOLDEN POTATO BAKE

Prepare enough packaged instant mashed potatoes for 4 servings, according to package directions, adding 1 teaspoon instant minced onion to cooking water. Fold in 1 cup cubed cooked carrots. Spoon into 4 individual casserole dishes. Top each with 1 tablespoon grated Parmesan cheese. Bake in a moderate oven (350°) for about 25 minutes or till golden brown. Makes 4 servings.

POTATO CLOUDS

Potatoes were never so light—

Packaged instant mashed potatoes (enough for 4 servings)

• • •

2 slightly beaten egg yolks
2 teaspoons snipped parsley
2 teaspoons instant minced onion

• • •

¼ cup sifted all-purpose flour
1 teaspoon baking powder
½ teaspoon salt
2 stiff-beaten egg whites

Prepare instant mashed potatoes using package directions; cool slightly. Stir in egg yolks, parsley, and onion. Sift together flour, baking powder, and salt. Add to potato mixture; mix well. Fold in stiff-beaten egg whites.

Drop by rounded tablespoons into deep hot fat (385°). Cook till puffs of potato are brown, turning once. Drain on absorbent towels. Keep hot in a slow oven (300°) while frying remaining puffs. Makes 2½ dozen.

HASHED-BROWN OMELET

New version of a potato classic!—

4 slices bacon
2 cups shredded cooked potatoes (or use packaged dry hash brown potatoes, cooked)
¼ cup chopped onion
¼ cup chopped green pepper

• • •

4 eggs
¼ cup milk
½ teaspoon salt
Dash pepper
1 cup shredded sharp process American cheese

Cook bacon till crisp in a 10- or 12-inch skillet. Leave drippings in skillet; remove bacon, and crumble. Mix potatoes, onion, and green pepper; pat into the skillet. Cook over low heat till underside is crisp and brown.

Blend eggs, milk, salt, and pepper; pour over browned potatoes. Top with shredded cheese and crumbled bacon. Cover; cook over low heat. When egg is done, carefully loosen omelet. Fold in half. Makes 4 servings.

CALIFORNIA POTATO BAKE

4 medium sweet potatoes

• • •

½ cup brown sugar
1 tablespoon cornstarch
¼ teaspoon salt
1 cup orange juice
¼ cup seedless raisins
¼ cup butter or margarine
3 tablespoons cooking sherry
2 tablespoons chopped California walnuts
½ teaspoon shredded orange peel

Cook potatoes in boiling salted water till tender; drain; peel, and halve lengthwise*. Arrange in shallow baking dish or pan. Sprinkle lightly with salt.

In a saucepan, mix brown sugar, cornstarch, and ¼ teaspoon salt. Blend in orange juice; add raisins. Cook and stir over high heat till mixture comes to boiling. Add remaining ingredients; pour over potatoes. Bake uncovered in a moderate oven (350°) for 20 minutes or till potatoes are well glazed. Makes 4 servings.

*Or if desired, use one 1-pound 2-ounce can (3 cups) sweet potatoes.

DIXIE DANDY

Make meal planning easy with this meat and potato dish—

1 1-pound can (2 cups) applesauce
¼ teaspoon ginger
1 12-ounce can luncheon meat, cut in 8 slices
Whole cloves
1 1-pound 2-ounce can (3 cups) sweet potatoes
½ cup apricot jam
½ teaspoon dry mustard
¼ teaspoon salt
1 tablespoon water

Combine applesauce and ginger; spread in a 10x6x1½-inch baking dish. Lightly score meat slices and stud each with whole cloves. Arrange potatoes and meat on applesauce.

Combine apricot jam, dry mustard, salt, and water; spread over meat and potatoes. Bake in hot oven (400°) for 25 minutes or till thoroughly heated. Makes 4 servings.

COTTAGE-FRIED SWEETS

3 slices bacon, cut in ½-inch pieces
¾ cup chopped onion
2½ cups diced canned sweet potatoes *or* 1½ pounds sweet potatoes, cooked and diced
1 teaspoon salt
½ teaspoon sugar

Cook bacon and onion till tender; add sweet potatoes, salt, and sugar. Cook uncovered over medium heat till potatoes are crispy on bottom; turn and cook other side. Serves 4.

POTATO-DATE BAKE

1 1-pound 2-ounce can sweet potatoes
¼ cup light cream
⅛ teaspoon cinnamon
½ teaspoon salt
½ cup chopped pitted dates
2 tablespoons butter or margarine, melted

Heat sweet potatoes; mash while hot. Add cream, cinnamon, salt, dates, and butter. Mix well and turn into a buttered 1-quart casserole. Bake at 350° for 20 to 25 minutes or till light brown. Makes 6 servings.

ORANGE BAKED SWEET POTATOES

5 or 6 medium sweet potatoes, cooked, peeled, and halved *or* 1 1-pound 2-ounce can sweet potatoes
1 peeled orange, thinly sliced
1 teaspoon shredded orange peel
⅔ cup dark corn syrup
¼ cup butter or margarine
½ teaspoon salt

Layer sweet potatoes and orange slices in a buttered 10x6x1½-inch baking dish. Combine remaining ingredients in small saucepan; bring to boiling; simmer uncovered for 5 minutes. Pour mixture over potatoes and orange slices. Bake in a moderate oven (350°) for 35 to 40 minutes, spooning sauce over potatoes several times. Serves 4 to 6.

BERRIED TREASURE PUFFS

1 1-pound 2-ounce can sweet potatoes
1 8¾-ounce can crushed pineapple, drained
1 egg
2 tablespoons butter or margarine
½ teaspoon salt
Dash pepper
Several dashes nutmeg
½ cup whole cranberry sauce

Whip sweet potatoes, pineapple, egg, butter, salt, pepper, and nutmeg till fluffy. Swirl cranberry sauce through potato mixture. Spoon into 6 greased custard cups. Bake in a moderate oven (375°) for about 40 minutes. Unmold and serve. Makes 6 servings.

MAPLE-FLAVORED SWEETS

6 medium sweet potatoes
½ cup maple-flavored syrup
1 tablespoon butter or margarine
1 teaspoon salt
½ cup apple cider or juice

Boil potatoes in jackets till nearly tender; peel and slice into a 10x6x1½-inch baking dish. Heat remaining ingredients to boiling; pour over potatoes and bake in moderate oven (350°) for 45 minutes, basting occasionally. Makes 6 to 8 servings.

CINNAMON APPLE YAMS

1 1-pound can (3 cups) vacuum packed sweet potatoes, cut in 1-inch slices
1 1-pound 1-ounce can (2 cups) applesauce
2 to 3 tablespoons brown sugar
2 tablespoons butter or margarine
½ teaspoon salt
2 tablespoons red cinnamon candies

Place *half* the sweet potatoes in a 1½-quart casserole dish. Top with *half* the applesauce. Repeat layers with remaining sweet potatoes and applesauce. Combine brown sugar, butter, and salt. Crumble over top. Sprinkle with red cinnamon candies. Bake, covered, at 350° for 45 minutes. Serves 6 to 8.

GLAZED SWEET POTATOES

1 3-ounce package orange-flavored gelatin
¼ cup brown sugar
Dash salt
1 cup boiling water
¼ cup butter or margarine
2 1-pound cans vacuum packed sweet potatoes

In a large skillet, dissolve gelatin, brown sugar, and salt in boiling water. Add butter and bring to boil, stirring constantly. Add potatoes; simmer about 15 minutes, basting frequently, till syrup thickens and potatoes are glazed. Serves 6 to 8.

POLYNESIAN CASSEROLE

1 1-pound 2-ounce can yams, drained and sliced
1 medium banana, thickly sliced
1 8¾-ounce can pineapple tidbits
¼ teaspoon salt
¼ cup flaked coconut

Arrange yams and bananas in a 10x6x1½-inch baking dish. Pour pineapple with syrup over all (be sure bananas are moistened). Sprinkle with salt. Bake at 350°, uncovered, for 15 minutes. Sprinkle with coconut; continue baking 15 minutes longer. Serves 4.

SPICED APRICOT SWEETS

1 1-pound 1-ounce can apricot halves
Whole cloves
1½ pounds sweet potatoes, cooked, peeled, and quartered
1 tablespoon sugar
1 tablespoon butter or margarine

Drain syrup from apricots into a 2-quart saucepan; add 3 whole cloves. Boil till reduced to ⅓ cup, about 8 to 10 minutes. Place *half* the sweet potatoes in bottom of 1½-quart casserole; top with *half* the apricots. Repeat layers. Stick a clove into each apricot half in the top layer. Pour reduced syrup over all; sprinkle with sugar and dot with butter. Bake in a moderate oven (350°) for 30 minutes. Makes 6 servings.

STUFFED YAMS

6 medium sweet potatoes or yams
1/4 cup butter or margarine, softened
1 tablespoon brown sugar
1 teaspoon salt
Dash pepper
Hot milk
1/4 cup chopped California walnuts

Scrub potatoes with a brush. Bake at 425° for 40 minutes or till done. (*Or*, if potatoes share oven, bake at 350° to 375° about 1 hour.) Cut slice from top of each. Scoop out inside, being careful not to break shell. Mash the potatoes in a mixing bowl.

Add butter, brown sugar, salt, pepper, and enough hot milk to moisten. Beat with electric mixer or rotary beater till fluffy. Fold in finely chopped nuts.

Pile mixture lightly into potato shells. If desired, garnish each with walnut half. Bake in a moderate oven (350°) for 15 to 20 minutes or till hot through. Serves 6.

PINEAPPLE SWEET POTATO CASSEROLE

1 1-pound 2-ounce can (3 cups) whole sweet potatoes
3 tablespoons butter or margarine
1/2 teaspoon salt
1/4 cup orange juice
1 8 3/4-ounce can (1 cup) crushed pineapple, drained

. . .

4 marshmallows, cut in half

Mash potatoes, add butter, salt, and orange juice; beat with electric or rotary beater until light and fluffy. Add crushed pineapple. Pour into greased 1-quart casserole. Dot with butter. Bake in a moderate oven (350°) about 45 minutes.

During last 10 or 15 minutes of baking, top casserole with halved marshmallows (walnut halves and pineapple spears, too, if desired). Bake until marshmallows are melted and golden. Makes 6 servings.

Twice baked and twice as good Stuffed Yams. Golden yams are scooped out and fluffed up with butter, milk, and brown sugar. Walnuts add tasty crunch as jackets are refilled.

TOASTED CROQUETTES

2 cups mashed cooked sweet potatoes
1 teaspoon salt
Dash pepper
1 tablespoon brown sugar
2 tablespoons butter, melted
12 marshmallows
Melted butter
½ cup fine dry bread crumbs

Mix first 5 ingredients. Shape mixture in balls around marshmallows. Roll in additional melted butter, then in crumbs. Fry in a skillet with 3 tablespoons melted butter till brown. Or, bake in shallow baking pan at 350° for 15 minutes. Makes 12.

SWEET POTATO BOATS

3 large sweet potatoes
½ cup cranberry-orange relish
¼ cup raisins
⅓ cup brown sugar
½ teaspoon salt
3 tablespoons butter or margarine
¼ cup California walnuts

Cook sweet potatoes in boiling, salted water until just tender. Remove skins. Cut in half lengthwise. Spoon out centers of sweet potato halves. Combine sweet potato centers and cranberry relish; beat till fluffy. Stir in raisins. Spoon mixture into potato halves.

Combine brown sugar and salt; cut in butter, then stir in nuts. Sprinkle over tops of sweet potatoes. Bake in a moderate oven (350°) for 30 minutes. Makes 6 servings.

CANDIED SWEETS

¼ cup butter or margarine
⅓ cup orange marmalade
2 tablespoons water
1 1-pound 2-ounce can (3 cups) sweet potatoes
Dash salt

Melt butter in skillet; stir in marmalade and water. Drain sweet potatoes; add to butter mixture. Dash with salt to taste. Heat, uncovered, over medium heat 10 to 15 minutes, basting frequently till potatoes are glazed and hot through. Makes 4 servings.

SWEET POTATO PUFF

2 cups hot mashed cooked sweet potatoes
½ cup milk
2 tablespoons butter or margarine
½ teaspoon salt
Dash allspice
½ teaspoon grated orange peel
2 egg yolks
2 egg whites

Combine potato, milk, butter, salt, allspice, and orange peel in a large mixing bowl. Beat with electric mixer or rotary beater till fluffy. Add egg yolks; beat well. Beat egg whites till stiff; carefully fold in potato mixture; turn into ungreased 1-quart souffle dish.

Bake in a moderate oven (350°) for 55 to 60 minutes, or till heated through. Serve with butter. Makes 6 servings.

AMBROSIA POTATO BAKE

½ lemon, thinly sliced
½ orange, thinly sliced
6 to 7 cups sliced, cooked *or* canned sweet potatoes, drained
1 8¾-ounce can (1 cup) crushed pineapple
½ cup brown sugar
½ cup butter, melted
½ teaspoon salt

• • •

½ cup shredded coconut
Maraschino cherries

Alternate lemon, orange, and sweet potato slices in an 11½x7½x1½-inch baking dish. Combine next 4 ingredients and pour over potatoes and fruit. Sprinkle coconut over top; garnish with cherries. Bake at 350° about 30 minutes. Serves 8 to 10.

FRENCH-FRIED SWEET POTATOES

Wash and pare 3 medium sweet potatoes. Slice uncooked potatoes in ½- to ¾-inch thick sticks; soak in iced water for 1 to 2 hours. Remove and dry between paper towels. Fry in deep hot fat (365°) till browned, 3 to 5 minutes; drain. Sprinkle with salt to taste. Makes about 4 cups.

spinach

What first induced man to pick and boil the leaves of this flavorful wild plant will probably remain a mystery. However, the existence of spinach is no longer left to the whims of nature. Now, a carefully cultivated crop, spinach thrives in fertile sandy fields during cool weather; as do other potherbs, mustard, kale, and collards.

When buying spinach, look for large fresh-appearing leaves with rich green color. Wilted or yellow leaves are telltale signs of having been too long for sale. Either variety, the crinkly leaf or the flat leaf, adds relish to a meal. Wash spinach well in a large pan of water; this method will settle any sand to pan bottom. Then lift it into a wire basket to drain. Wrap leaves in paper or cloth towels, store in vegetable crisper. The sooner used, the more delectable this fragile green is.

The tale of why man first ate these tender leaves may be speculative, but this is fact—spinach cooked without water except that which clings to the leaves, preserves a flavor essence and fine texture that make it a joy to the epicure.

SPINACH ELEGANTE

Sour cream and sharp cheese dazzle the topping of this snappy dish—

2 10-ounce packages frozen chopped spinach
3 slices bacon, cooked and crumbled
1 6-ounce can ($1\frac{1}{3}$ cups) broiled sliced mushrooms, drained
Dash pepper
$\frac{1}{4}$ teaspoon marjoram
1 cup dairy sour cream
$\frac{1}{2}$ cup shredded sharp process American cheese

Cook spinach according to package directions. Drain well; spread on bottom of 10x-6x$1\frac{1}{2}$-inch baking dish. Arrange bacon and mushrooms over spinach in casserole. Sprinkle with pepper and marjoram.

Bake in slow oven (325°) for 15 minutes. Cover with sour cream and top with cheese. Return to oven about 5 minutes or till cheese melts. Makes 6 servings.

SPINACH RAMEKINS

Perfect molded vegetable dish for your next special dinner party—

2 10-ounce packages frozen chopped spinach
Milk
$\frac{1}{3}$ cup chopped onion
3 slightly beaten eggs
2 tablespoons butter or margarine, melted
$1\frac{1}{4}$ teaspoons salt
Dash pepper

Thaw spinach until it can be broken apart with fork. Place in saucepan; cover and bring to boiling; cook only until completely thawed. Drain, reserving liquid. (Press lightly while draining.)

Measure liquid and add enough milk to make $1\frac{1}{2}$ cups. Add spinach and remaining ingredients; mix well. Spoon into 6 to 8 greased custard cups, distributing liquid.

Set custard cups in shallow pan, filling pan to 1 inch with hot water. Bake in moderate oven (350°) for 50 to 60 minutes, or till mixture doesn't adhere to knife. Unmold and serve. Makes 6 to 8 servings.

CREME D' EPINARDS (Creamed Spinach)

1 pound fresh spinach, cooked
$\frac{1}{4}$ cup medium white sauce
$\frac{1}{2}$ teaspoon salt
Dash pepper
Dash Worcestershire sauce
Dash bottled hot pepper sauce
$\frac{1}{4}$ cup Hollandaise sauce

Chop and drain spinach; add white sauce, salt, pepper, Worcestershire sauce, and bottled hot pepper sauce; mix thoroughly. Spread into an 8-inch pie plate and top with Hollandaise sauce. Brown lightly in hot oven (425°) for 15 minutes. Serves 4.

FRANKS FLORENTINE

Franks snuggle into fluffy rice and cheese atop spinach—goes together in a wink—

1 10-ounce package frozen chopped spinach, cooked and drained
$1\frac{1}{2}$ cups cooked rice
1 11-ounce can condensed Cheddar cheese soup
$\frac{1}{4}$ cup milk
2 tablespoons minced onion
$\frac{1}{2}$ pound (4 to 5) frankfurters halved crosswise

Spread spinach in bottom of 10x6x$1\frac{1}{2}$-inch baking dish. Combine rice, soup, milk, and onion; spoon over spinach.

Score halved franks with an X-shaped cut; arrange on casserole, pressing into rice. Bake at 375° for 20 to 25 minutes or till heated through. Makes 4 servings.

SPINACH DELICIOUS

1 10-ounce package frozen chopped spinach
2 tablespoons butter or margarine
$\frac{1}{4}$ cup light cream
2 tablespoons prepared horseradish
$\frac{1}{2}$ teaspoon salt
Dash pepper

Cook spinach according to package directions; drain. Add remaining ingredients; mix well and heat through. Serves 4 or 5.

SPINACH IN TOMATO CUPS

Luscious fresh tomatoes brimming with rich, creamy spinach—

6 medium tomatoes
Salt
½ cup light cream
1 egg yolk
12 ounces fresh spinach, cooked, chopped, and drained (¾ cup)
3 tablespoons butter or margarine melted

Cut top (¼ inch) off each tomato. Empty inside completely of juice and seeds, but not fruit. Sprinkle inside with salt. Combine cream and egg yolk; add chopped spinach and *1 tablespoon* of the butter. Salt to taste.

Heat and stir *just* to simmering. Fill tomatoes solid with the creamed spinach. Place in 10x6x1½-inch baking dish. Top each with *1 teaspoon* melted butter. Bake in moderate oven (375°) for 20 minutes. Serves 6.

SPINACH-CARROT MEDLEY

5 medium carrots, sliced (1½ cups)
1 medium onion, sliced
1 10- or 12-ounce package frozen leaf spinach
3 tablespoons butter or margarine
3 tablespoons all-purpose flour
1½ cups milk
1 cup shredded sharp process American cheese
¼ teaspoon salt
Dash pepper
½ cup buttered soft bread crumbs

Cook carrots and onions covered in small amount boiling salted water till almost tender, about 8 minutes. Cook spinach according to package directions. Drain vegetables.

Meanwhile, melt butter in saucepan. Blend in flour; add milk all at once. Cook, stirring constantly, till mixture thickens and bubbles. Remove from heat; add cheese, salt, and pepper, stirring till cheese melts.

Place *half* the spinach in ungreased 1-quart casserole. Cover with *half* the carrots and onions; top with *half* the sauce. Repeat layers. Sprinkle with bread crumbs. Bake in moderate oven (350°) for 15 to 20 minutes or till crumbs are golden brown. Serves 6.

SPINACH DELIGHT

Ideal for a buffet dinner—fix ahead and bake just before serving—

2 10-ounce packages frozen chopped spinach, cooked and drained
4 slices bacon, cooked and crumbled
1 5-ounce can (⅔ cup) water chestnuts, drained and sliced
1 10-ounce package frozen Welsh rarebit, thawed (about 1 cup)
1 cup canned French-fried onions

Place cooked spinach in 10x6x1½-inch baking dish. Top with bacon and water chestnuts. Spread Welsh rarebit evenly over top. Garnish with French-fried onions. Bake in moderate oven (350°) for 20 to 25 minutes or till heated through. Serves 6 to 8.

SPINACH WITH MUSHROOMS

½ clove garlic, minced
½ cup sliced fresh mushrooms *or* 1 3-ounce can (⅔ cup) broiled sliced mushrooms, drained
1 tablespoon butter or margarine
2 pounds fresh spinach, chopped *or* 2 10- or 12-ounce packages frozen leaf spinach, thawed
1 teaspoon lemon juice
Salt and pepper

Cook garlic and mushrooms in butter 2 to 3 minutes; add spinach and cover. Reduce heat when steam forms; cook 3 to 10 minutes. Add lemon juice; season to taste with salt and pepper. Makes 4 servings.

CHINESE SPINACH

1 pound fresh spinach
2 tablespoons salad oil
1 tablespoon soy sauce

Wash and pat dry spinach leaves. Remove stems and cut into 1-inch pieces. Tear spinach leaves into bite-size pieces. Heat oil and soy in skillet; add spinach. Cover and cook about 1 minutes or till just wilted. Uncover and toss spinach till tender-crisp and well coated, about 2 minutes. Serves 4.

GERMAN STYLE SPINACH

1 pound fresh spinach
8 slices bacon
¼ cup finely chopped onion
3 tablespoons vinegar
½ teaspoon salt
Dash pepper
1 hard-cooked egg, sliced

Wash spinach well; with water clinging to leaves, place in saucepan with no added water and steam 8 to 10 minutes. Drain. Meanwhile, cook bacon till crisp; drain, reserving 1 tablespoon fat. Crumble bacon.

Cook onion in reserved fat till tender but not brown; add to spinach with bacon, vinegar, salt, and pepper. Toss lightly. Garnish with egg slices. Makes 4 servings.

SPINACH-POTATO BAKE

1 10¼-ounce can frozen condensed cream of potato soup, thawed *or* 1 10½-ounce can condensed cream of potato soup
1 10-ounce package frozen chopped spinach, thawed
2 beaten eggs
1 teaspoon instant minced onion
Dash salt
Dash pepper

Combine all ingredients, mixing well. Turn into lightly greased 10x6x1½-inch baking dish. Bake uncovered in moderate oven (350°) for 30 minutes. Makes 4 to 6 servings.

SPINACH SUPREME

2 10-ounce packages frozen chopped spinach
1½ cups milk
2 slightly beaten eggs
1 1¾-ounce envelope dry cream of leek soup mix

Cook spinach according to package directions; drain thoroughly. Combine milk and eggs; gradually stir into the soup mix. Add spinach and mix well. Turn into 10x6x1½-inch baking dish. Bake in moderate oven (350°) for 30 minutes, or until edges of casserole are set, but center, creamy. Serves 6 to 8.

HERBED SPINACH BAKE

A hint of herb mingled with rice and spinach baked in a rich custard—

1 10-ounce package frozen chopped spinach
1 cup cooked rice
1 cup shredded sharp process American cheese
2 slightly beaten eggs
⅓ cup milk
2 tablespoons butter or margarine, softened
2 tablespoons chopped onion
1 teaspoon salt
½ teaspoon Worcestershire sauce
¼ teaspoon rosemary, crushed *or* thyme leaves, crushed

Cook spinach according to package directions; drain. Mix in remaining ingredients. Pour into 10x6x1½-inch baking dish.

Bake in moderate oven (350°) for 20 to 25 minutes or till knife inserted halfway between center and edge comes out clean. Cut in squares to serve. Makes 6 servings.

SPINACH-CARROT CUSTARD

Perfect for your next oven-roast meal—

¼ cup butter or margarine
¼ cup all-purpose flour
1½ cups milk
1 tablespoon instant minced onion
½ teaspoon salt

• • •

2 slightly beaten eggs
1½ cups shredded carrots, cooked and drained
1 10-ounce package frozen chopped spinach, cooked and drained

Melt butter in saucepan; blend in flour; add milk, onion, and salt. Cook, stirring constantly, until mixture thickens and bubbles; remove from heat. Stir small amount hot sauce into eggs; return to hot mixture and cook till blended, stirring constantly.

Add carrots and spinach. Pour into eight 5-ounce custard cups. Bake in slow oven (325°) for 20 to 25 minutes, or till knife inserted halfway between center and edge comes out clean. Makes 8 servings.

6
12
10
11

squash

Like maize and tomatoes, squash is a native of the Western hemisphere and was well known to the American Indians. Botanically, the squash family is divided into two groups, winter and summer.

Winter squash thrive in hot summer weather, are harvested in fall, and stored over the winter—hence the name. When buying winter squash, look for hard rinds and squash which are heavy for their size. Winter squash are adapted for long storage if kept in a dry place at a moderate temperature. The large green and red squash pictured in left background is a turban, as is the large cut squash. Resting against the top of the turban is a creamy-colored butternut squash. Below is the widely ribbed orange or green acorn squash.

Summer squash are quick-growing fruits which are eaten when immature. In choosing summer squash, look for small, young squash that are heavy for their size. The rind should be soft enough to yield easily to thumbnail pressure—hard rinds on summer squash indicate mature fruits with stringy flesh. Summer squash should be refrigerated and used as soon as possible to prevent spoilage. Pattypans are the mushroom-shaped, green squash with scalloped edges pictured in the foreground. The cylindrical-shaped, green striped squash at the right is zucchini. A yellow crookneck squash leans against the zucchini.

ZUCCHINI SUPREME

Flavorful blend of vegetable favorites—

4 cups sliced, unpared zucchini
1 medium onion, thinly sliced and separated into rings
3 medium tomatoes, peeled and sliced
½ cup chopped green pepper
1 8-ounce package sliced process American cheese
3 cups ½-inch caraway rye bread cubes
¼ cup butter or margarine, melted

Alternate layers of zucchini, onion, tomato, and green pepper in 13x9x2-inch baking dish; season. Cut cheese slices in half diagonally; place atop casserole. Sprinkle with bread cubes; drizzle with butter.

Cover and bake in moderate oven (350°) for 45 minutes; uncover and bake 15 minutes longer or till tender. Serves 8 to 10.

CROOKNECK CURRY

Cut 3 medium crookneck squash crosswise into ¼-inch slices. Cook in small amount boiling salted water until almost tender, about 8 minutes; drain.

Combine ⅓ cup light cream, ¼ to ½ teaspoon curry powder, ¼ teaspoon salt, and dash pepper. Add squash and heat through. Serve in sauce dishes. Makes 6 servings.

GARDEN VEGETABLE BOWL

¼ cup butter or margarine
4 cups sliced unpared zucchini squash (about 1 pound)
1½ cups cut fresh, frozen, or drained canned whole-kernel corn
½ cup chopped onion
⅓ cup chopped green pepper
½ teaspoon salt
1 tablespoon fresh snipped dill *or* 1 teaspoon dried

Melt butter in skillet; add zucchini, corn, onion, and green pepper. Sprinkle with salt. Cover and cook, stirring occasionally, 10 to 12 minutes, or till vegetables are tender. Sprinkle with dill. Serves 4 to 6.

ZUCCHINI FLORENTINE

Little slices of bright green squash baked in a well-seasoned custard—

6 small zucchini, cut in ¼-inch slices
2 tablespoons butter or margarine
1 cup evaporated milk
3 slightly beaten eggs
1 teaspoon salt
¼ teaspoon pepper
¼ teaspoon garlic salt
¼ teaspoon paprika

Place zucchini in 1½-quart casserole; dot with butter. Bake in hot oven (400°) for 15 minutes or till zucchini is partially cooked but still crisp. Combine next 5 ingredients and pour over zucchini. Sprinkle with paprika. Set casserole in shallow pan, filling pan to 1 inch with hot water.

Bake in moderate oven (350°) for 40 minutes, or till knife inserted halfway between center and edge comes out clean. Serves 6.

SPANISH ZUCCHINI

1½ teaspoons salt
1 teaspoon monosodium glutamate
½ teaspoon chili powder
Dash pepper

• • •

4 pork chops, ½-inch thick
½ cup uncooked rice
1 1-pound 13-ounce can tomatoes
½ cup chopped green pepper
½ cup chopped onion
½ cup chopped ripe olives
1 tablespoon sugar
2 cups thinly sliced unpared zucchini squash
¼ cup grated Parmesan cheese

Mix first 4 ingredients. Trim fat from chops and heat in skillet. Remove trimmings and brown chops, seasoning with *1 teaspoon* of the chili mixture. Drain off fat. Add rice, tomatoes, green pepper, onion, olives, and sugar. Border with zucchini; sprinkle all with remaining chili mixture.

Cover; cook, stirring occasionally, 1 hour or till pork is done—no pink showing when cut near bone. Top with Parmesan cheese; cover to melt. Makes 4 servings.

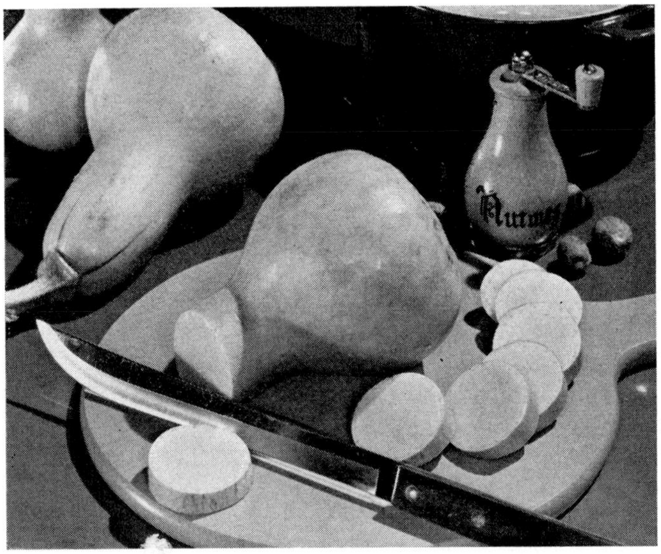

BUTTERNUT BAKE

Cut 3 pounds butternut squash in half; remove seeds. Bake cut side down in hot oven (400°) for 45 minutes or till tender. Scoop out pulp; add 2 tablespoons butter, 2 teaspoons brown sugar, and ¼ teaspoon salt; beat. Stir in ¼ cup light raisins and 1 tablespoon chopped pecans. Turn into 1-quart casserole. Combine 1 tablespoon *each* butter, brown sugar, and light corn syrup; drizzle over top of squash. Sprinkle with 1 tablespoon chopped pecans. Bake at 350° for about 25 minutes. Serves 4 to 6.

DELICATA BAKE

Quarter 2 delicata squash; seed. Bake in shallow pan at 350° about 40 minutes or till almost tender. Form 1 pound pork sausage into 24 balls; brown in skillet; drain.

Mix one 1-pound 1-ounce can applesauce and 1 teaspoon cinnamon. Season squash; top squash with applesauce, then sausage. Bake 20 minutes. Serves 8.

SPICED TURBAN SQUASH

2 small turban squash
¼ cup honey
2 tablespoons butter or margarine, melted
1 teaspoon salt
½ teaspoon ginger
¼ teaspoon nutmeg
Dash pepper

Cut squash in quarters; remove seeds. Place cut side down in shallow baking dish. Bake in moderate oven (375°) for 30 minutes. Turn cut side up. Combine remaining ingredients; spoon over squash. Bake 25 to 30 minutes longer or till squash is tender. Serves 8.

ZUCCHINI CHINESE STYLE

2 slices bacon
3 medium unpared zucchini, scored with fork and sliced diagonally
1/4 cup chicken broth
2 teaspoons cornstarch
1/2 teaspoon monosodium glutamate
1/2 teaspoon salt
2 teaspoons cold water

Cook bacon till crisp; remove from skillet. Add sliced zucchini to bacon drippings in skillet; toss to coat. Pour chicken broth over zucchini. Cover and steam 4 to 5 minutes till squash is almost tender.

Blend cornstarch, monosodium glutamate, and salt with cold water; stir into zucchini mixture. Cook, stirring constantly, till mixture boils. Turn into serving dish; garnish with crumbled bacon. Serves 4 or 5.

BABY CROOKNECK SQUASH

Select little yellow summer squashes, less than 3 inches long. Steam till tender. Split lengthwise and brush cut surfaces generously with melted butter or margarine.

Season with salt and pepper. Sprinkle liberally with snipped parsley and chopped canned pimiento. Place squash halves in shallow pan; heat in moderate oven (350°) just till they sizzle. Serve piping hot.

CHEESE-TOPPED ZUCCHINI

3 medium zucchini squash
1 medium onion, thinly sliced
1 tablespoon salad oil
1/2 to 1 teaspoon crushed oregano
1 8-ounce can (1 cup) tomato sauce
1 6- or 8-ounce package sliced Mozzarella cheese
Grated Parmesan cheese

Cut zucchini in half lengthwise. In a large skillet, cook onion in hot salad oil till tender but not brown. Add zucchini halves, cut side up; sprinkle with salt, pepper, and oregano. Pour tomato sauce over.

Cover; cook just till tender, about 10 minutes. Top zucchini with cheese slices; sprinkle with oregano, if desired. Pass Parmesan cheese. Makes 6 servings.

SAUSAGE-ZUCCHINI BOATS

Cheese tops zesty sausage filling—

4 medium zucchini (2 pounds)
1/4 pound bulk pork sausage
1/4 cup chopped onion
1/2 cup grated Parmesan cheese
1/2 cup fine cracker crumbs
1 slightly beaten egg
1/2 teaspoon monosodium glutamate
1/4 teaspoon salt
1/4 teaspoon thyme
Dash garlic salt
Dash pepper

Cook whole zucchini in boiling salted water till barely tender, 7 to 10 minutes. Cut in half lengthwise; scoop squash from shells and mash. Cook sausage and onion; drain off excess fat. Stir in mashed zucchini. Reserve *2 tablespoons* Parmesan cheese; mix in remaining ingredients.

Spoon into zucchini shells; place in shallow baking dish. Sprinkle with reserved Parmesan cheese; dash with paprika. Bake in moderate oven (350°) for 25 to 30 minutes, or till heated through. Serves 4.

SAUCY ZUCCHINI

1 pound unpared zucchini, thinly sliced (about 4 cups)
2 medium onions, thinly sliced (about 1 cup)
2 tablespoons butter or margarine
2 tablespoons all-purpose flour
1 teaspoon salt
Dash pepper
1 cup milk

• • •

1/2 cup shredded sharp process cheese
1/2 cup buttered bread crumbs

Cook zucchini and onion in small amount boiling water till tender. In a saucepan melt butter; blend in flour, salt, and pepper. Add milk all at once; cook, stirring constantly, until mixture thickens and bubbles. Combine sauce with cooked vegetables.

Place in a 10x6x1 1/2-inch baking dish. Top with shredded cheese and then buttered crumbs. Bake in moderate oven (350°) for about 25 minutes. Makes 4 to 6 servings.

BAKED BANANA SQUASH

Cut 3 pounds banana squash into serving portions; remove seeds. Place skin side up in baking dish; pour ⅓ cup hot water in dish. Bake in moderate oven (375°) for 20 minutes, or till almost tender.

Turn squash skin side down. Combine ½ cup brown sugar, ¼ cup soft butter or margarine, and 1 teaspoon paprika; spread over squash. Continue baking about 5 to 10 minutes or till squash is tender, basting frequently to glaze. To serve, pass extra butter. Makes 8 servings.

ACORN ELEGANTE

Halve and seed 3 acorn squash; bake at 350° for 35 minutes. Cook 2 cups chopped onion in 3 tablespoons butter. Add one 6-ounce can sliced mushrooms, drained, and 2 tablespoons snipped parsley. Season and stuff squash. Bake 20 minutes. Top with 1 cup shredded process cheese and 1 tablespoon buttered cornflake crumbs; bake till cheese melts. Serves 6.

HUBBARD SQUASH SQUARES IN SOUR CREAM

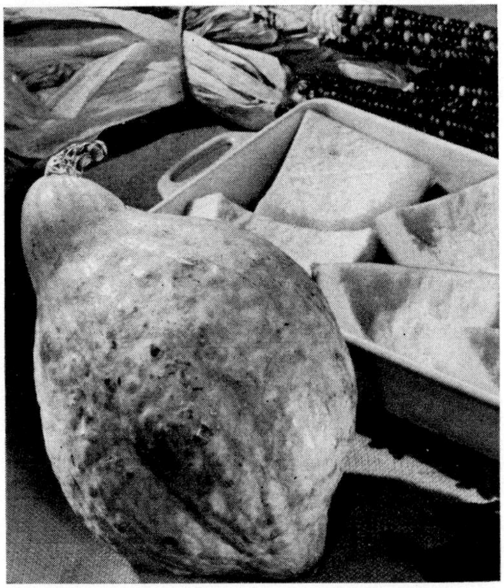

4 cups cubed, pared Hubbard squash
2 tablespoons chopped green onion including tops
1 tablespoon butter or margarine
½ cup dairy sour cream
2 tablespoons milk
½ teaspoon salt
½ teaspoon dill weed

Cook squash in boiling salted water 10 minutes or till tender; drain well and sprinkle with pepper. Meanwhile, cook onion in butter till tender but not brown; blend in sour cream, milk, salt, and dash pepper; heat. Place hot cooked squash on platter; pour cream mixture over. Sprinkle with dill weed. Serves 4 to 6.

SQUASH DELIGHT

2 medium acorn squash
2 tablespoons butter or margarine
½ cup diced fully cooked ham
2 tablespoons chopped green pepper
2 tablespoons chopped celery
1½ tablespoons all-purpose flour
¾ cup milk
2 tablespoons sliced stuffed olives
2 hard cooked eggs, chopped
½ teaspoon salt
Dash pepper
1 tablespoon butter or margarine, melted
⅓ cup fine dry bread crumbs

Cut squash in half; remove seeds. Bake, cut side down, in shallow pan in moderate oven (350°) for 35 to 45 minutes till tender. Meanwhile, melt 2 tablespoons butter; cook ham, green pepper, and celery till tender.

Blend in flour; add milk all at once. Cook, stirring constantly, until mixture thickens and bubbles. Add olives, hard cooked eggs, salt, and pepper. Spoon mixture into cavities of squash. Combine 1 tablespoon butter and bread crumbs; sprinkle over top. Bake at 350° for 15 minutes longer. Serves 4.

HERB STUFFED SQUASH

3 acorn squash
1 slightly beaten egg
1 chicken bouillon cube
⅓ cup boiling water
¼ cup chopped onion
2 tablespoons butter or margarine
½ cup crushed herb-seasoned stuffing
½ teaspoon salt
Dash pepper

Cut squash in half lengthwise; remove seeds. Place cut side down on baking sheet. Bake in hot oven (400°) for 30 minutes or till tender. Remove squash from shells; mash. Add egg and bouillon cube dissolved in water.

Cook onion in butter till tender but not brown; stir in stuffing. Reserve ¼ cup stuffing mixture; stir remainder into squash. Season with salt and pepper. Spoon squash mixture into shells. Top with reserved stuffing. Bake in hot oven (400°) for 25 to 30 minutes till lightly browned. Serves 6.

GLAZED SQUASH RINGS

Attractive squash rings double as a vegetable and meat platter garnish—

2 acorn squash
Salt and pepper
⅔ cup brown sugar
¼ cup soft butter or margarine

Trim ends and cut squash crosswise in 1-inch slices; discard seeds. Cut slices in half; season to taste. Arrange in single layer in large shallow baking dish; cover and bake in moderate oven (350°) for 30 to 35 minutes or till squash is almost tender.

Combine brown sugar and butter; spread over squash. Continue baking, uncovered, for 15 to 20 minutes or till squash is glazed, basting occasionally. Serves 6.

SQUASH CHIPS

Potato chips never tasted this good—

Acorn squash
Salt
Ginger

Peel and seed squash. Slice tissue paper thin as for potato chips. Soak in ice water for 1 hour. Drain and pat dry. Fry in deep hot fat (360°) until brown. Drain on paper towels; sprinkle with salt and ginger.

FRUIT-FILLED SQUASH

Apple and orange spice the stuffing—

3 medium acorn squash
½ teaspoon salt
3 cups chopped apple
1 medium orange, peeled and diced
½ cup brown sugar
¼ cup butter or margarine, melted

Cut squash in half crosswise; remove seeds. Place cut side down in shallow baking dish. Bake in moderate oven (350°) for 35 minutes. Turn cut sides up; sprinkle with salt. Combine apple, orange, brown sugar, and butter; fill squash with mixture. Continue baking at 350° for 25 minutes or till tender. Makes 6 servings.

Acorn squash features onions and walnuts for the tasty filling and a spicy molasses glaze glistening on top. This splendid blend of flavors adds a festive touch to any meal.

GLAZED SQUASH WITH ONIONS AND WALNUTS

Cut 3 acorn squash in half lengthwise; remove seeds. Bake cut side down in shallow pan at 350° for 35 to 40 minutes or till almost tender. Turn cut side up; season.

Fill cavities with 2 cups drained cooked or canned small onions and ½ cup broken walnuts. Melt ⅓ cup butter or margarine; add ⅓ cup light molasses, ¼ teaspoon salt, and ¼ teaspoon cinnamon; spoon over squash and filling. Continue baking 15 to 20 minutes or till squash is tender, brushing occasionally with sauce to glaze. Serves 6.

DILLY SQUASH

1 pound yellow summer squash
2 tablespoons butter or margarine
1 tablespoon fresh snipped parsley
¼ teaspoon dill weed
¼ teaspoon salt
Dash onion powder

Slice squash crosswise ¼-inch thick. Melt butter in skillet. Add squash, parsley, dill weed, salt, and onion powder. Cover and cook over low heat for 8 to 10 minutes or till tender, stirring occasionally. Serve piping hot. Makes 4 to 6 servings.

tomatoes

Behold a sun worshipper! Each dainty yellow blossom of the tomato vine promises juicy goodness, whether it becomes a giant or matures into a tiny cherry tomato. Is the tomato a fruit or a vegetable? The French first termed it *pomme d'amour* (apple of love), and then there's the story about Sir Walter Raleigh giving Queen Elizabeth a tomato as a token of affection. Horticulturally, the tomato is not only a fruit, but a giant berry. Today, however, we use this succulent red fruit as a vegetable in a hundred ways. Tossed salads aren't quite the same without fresh tomato wedges, not to mention the bacon, lettuce, and tomato institution, or pizza and tomato soup. Creole cooking exists only because of tomatoes, and our South American neighbors have depended upon them for centuries.

In use, tomatoes deserve loving care, whether stewed, fried, scalloped, broiled, or baked. Since cold surroundings stop their ripening, the place for tomatoes is in the refrigerator—right up to the time they're to be served or cooked. When the occasion calls for peeling fresh tomatoes, next time try this slick trick: dip the whole tomato into boiling water for just a minute, then plunge in cold water. Surprisingly the skin slips right off, leaving a firm, whole tomato.

HERBED TOMATOES

Peel 6 medium ripe tomatoes; place in a deep bowl. In a jar, combine 2/3 cup salad oil, 1/4 cup vinegar, 1/4 cup snipped parsley, 1/4 cup sliced green onions, 1 teaspoon salt, 1/4 teaspoon freshly ground pepper, 2 teaspoons snipped fresh thyme or marjoram leaves, *or* 1/2 teaspoon dried thyme or marjoram, and 1 clove garlic, minced. Shake well and pour over peeled tomatoes. Cover and chill at least several hours or overnight, occasionally spooning the dressing over.

At serving time, spoon herb dressing over tomatoes again. Then transfer tomatoes to serving platter. Serves 6.

CORN-STUFFED TOMATOES

Goes with dinner, or stars in a luncheon—

4 large firm ripe tomatoes
2 medium ears sweet corn, cooked and cut off cob (1 cup kernels)
1/4 cup chopped green onions
1/3 cup chopped green pepper
2 tablespoons chopped canned pimiento
1/2 teaspoon salt

• • •

3 tablespoons olive oil
1 tablespoon lemon juice or vinegar
1 small clove garlic, minced
Salt and freshly ground pepper to taste

Cut out tomato cores. Cut each tomato, *not quite all the way through,* into wedges. Spoon out and reserve centers. Invert tomato cups to drain; chill. Chop tomato pulp fine; drain. Mix chopped tomato, corn, onions, green pepper, pimiento, and salt. Combine remaining ingredients for dressing; pour over vegetables and mix well. Chill thoroughly. At serving time, spoon mixture into chilled tomato cups. Serve on salad greens; pass mayonnaise. Makes 4 servings.

CHEESE TOMATO PIES

1 cup canned tomatoes
1 6-ounce can (2/3 cup) tomato paste
1/2 teaspoon garlic salt
1/2 teaspoon salt
Dash pepper
1 teaspoon oregano

• • •

1/2 cup milk
2 tablespoons melted butter
2 cups packaged biscuit mix
1 12-ounce carton (1 1/2 cups) cottage cheese
6 tablespoons grated Parmesan cheese

Combine canned tomatoes and tomato paste; stir in seasonings. Add milk and butter to biscuit mix; stir quickly with a fork until dry ingredients are just moistened. Knead gently a few seconds; divide into 6 pieces.

Pat each piece into a 6-inch circle on lightly greased baking sheets. Pinch up edges to make slight rims. Spread cottage cheese on circles; cover with tomato mixture. Sprinkle 1 tablespoon Parmesan cheese over each pie. Bake in hot oven (425°) for 10 minutes. Reduce heat to 350°. Bake 10 minutes longer. Makes 6 individual pies.

SCALLOPED TOMATOES

1 cup diced celery
½ cup finely chopped onion
2 tablespoons butter or margarine
2 tablespoons all-purpose flour
1 1-pound 12-ounce can tomatoes
3 slices bread, toasted
1 tablespoon sugar
1 teaspoon salt
Dash pepper
2 teaspoons prepared mustard

Cook celery and onion in butter until just tender; blend in flour. Butter toast; cut in ½-inch cubes. In 1½-quart casserole, combine the onion-celery mixture with tomatoes, *half* the toast cubes, the sugar, and seasonings. Bake at 350° for 30 minutes. Top casserole with remaining toast cubes and bake 20 minutes longer. Serves 8.

ORIENTAL SKILLET

Melt 2 tablespoons butter or margarine in skillet; add ½ cup chopped onion, and 2 medium unpared zucchini squash, cut in quarters. Cover; cook over medium heat 5 minutes. Stir in 3 medium tomatoes, cut in wedges, one 3-ounce can (⅔ cup) broiled sliced mushrooms, drained, ¼ teaspoon *each* salt, curry powder, and ginger, and dash freshly ground pepper. Cover and cook 5 minutes longer or till vegetables are tender but slightly crisp. Serves 4 to 6.

TOMATO CASSEROLE

1 medium onion, chopped
2 tablespoons butter or margarine
4 medium ripe tomatoes, sliced
1 cup shredded sharp process American cheese
1 cup fine soft bread crumbs
1 cup dairy sour cream
2 well beaten eggs
½ teaspoon salt

Cook onions in butter till tender. Place *half* the tomatoes in 10x6x1½-inch baking dish. Top with *half each* onions, cheese, and crumbs; repeat. Mix remaining ingredients. Pour over top; cover. Bake at 350° for 30 minutes. Uncover; bake 10 minutes. Serves 6.

FRIED TOMATOES

Cut unpared *green* tomatoes in ½-inch slices. Dip into flour, salt, and pepper. Fry slowly in small amount hot fat until browned. Turn and brown on other side.

For *ripe* tomatoes, dip ½-inch slices into beaten egg mixed with water, then crumbs; fry quickly in hot fat; salt and pepper.

BAKED TOMATOES WITH FRENCH DRESSING

4 medium ripe tomatoes
¼ cup salad oil
1½ tablespoons cider vinegar
¼ teaspoon Worcestershire sauce
1 tablespoon sugar
1½ teaspoons instant minced onion
¼ teaspoon salt
¼ teaspoon dry mustard
⅓ cup medium fine cracker crumbs
1 tablespoon butter or margarine, melted

Cut thin slice from top of each tomato. Hollow out slightly. Combine next 7 ingredients. Spoon into center of each tomato. Mix cracker crumbs and butter. Sprinkle over tomatoes. Place in a 9x1½-inch round baking pan. Bake at 350° for 30 minutes or till heated through. Serves 4.

SPICY WHOLE TOMATOES

¼ cup butter or margarine
½ cup chopped onion
2 tablespoons brown sugar
6 whole cloves
2 bay leaves, crumbled
2 inches stick cinnamon, broken in pieces
1½ teaspoons salt
Dash freshly ground pepper
6 medium ripe tomatoes, peeled and cored

Melt butter in skillet; add next 7 ingredients; cook till onion is tender. Add tomatoes, cored side down; spoon butter mixture over. Cover; simmer 5 minutes. Carefully turn tomatoes. Simmer uncovered 5 to 10 minutes longer or till tender, basting often. Serve in sauce dishes. Makes 6 servings.

The creamy sauce pictured here makes Dill Tomatoes a celebrity. A combination of sour cream and dill tops plump broiled tomatoes.

What could be more colorful or delicious with steaks or chops than hot juicy tomato halves and this elegant sauce.

DILL TOMATOES

½ cup dairy sour cream
¼ cup mayonnaise or salad dressing
2 tablespoons finely chopped onion
1 teaspoon snipped fresh dill weed *or* ¼ teaspoon dried
¼ teaspoon salt
4 large firm ripe tomatoes

Combine first 5 ingredients; mix well. Chill. Core tomatoes; cut in half crosswise. Season cut surfaces with salt and pepper; dot with butter or margarine. Broil, cut side up, 3 inches from heat about 5 minutes or till hot through (don't turn). Top with chilled sauce. Makes 8 servings.

BAKED TOMATOES

2 medium ripe tomatoes
1 teaspoon prepared mustard

• • •

¼ cup minced onion
¼ cup buttered soft bread crumbs
½ teaspoon Worcestershire sauce
Dash salt

Remove stems from tomatoes; halve crosswise. Arrange in a 10x6x1½-inch baking dish, cut sides up. Spread with mustard; combine onion, bread crumbs, Worcestershire sauce, and salt. Sprinkle over tomatoes. Bake in a moderate oven (375°) for 20 minutes or till heated through. Serves 4.

TOMATOES AND OKRA

1½ cups fresh okra, cut in ½-inch slices*

• • •

½ cup chopped onion
½ cup chopped green pepper
2 tablespoons salad oil
1 tablespoon sugar
1 teaspoon all-purpose flour
¾ teaspoon salt
¼ teaspoon pepper
3 tomatoes, peeled and quartered, *or* 1 cup canned tomatoes

Cook okra covered in small amount boiling salted water 10 minutes; drain.

Cook chopped onion and green pepper in salad oil till tender but not brown; blend in sugar, flour, salt, and pepper. Add tomatoes and okra; cook over low heat till vegetables are hot through, stirring as little as possible. Makes 4 servings.

*Or use one 10-ounce package frozen okra. Cook according to package directions.

HOT HERBED TOMATOES

Bright tomatoes cook gently in flavorful herb-butter sauce—

¼ cup butter or margarine
1 teaspoon brown sugar
½ teaspoon salt
½ teaspoon monosodium glutamate
Dash pepper
4 or 5 firm ripe medium tomatoes, cored and peeled

• • •

¼ cup finely chopped celery
2 tablespoons finely snipped parsley
2 tablespoons finely snipped chives
½ teaspoon crushed oregano (optional)

In skillet, melt butter; add brown sugar, salt, monosodium glutamate, and pepper. Add tomatoes, cored side down. Cover; cook gently 5 minutes. Carefully turn tomatoes; spoon butter mixture over. Add remaining ingredients to sauce and cook uncovered 5 minutes longer; spoon sauce over tomatoes before serving. Makes 4 or 5 servings.

POMODORI RIPIENI
(Stuffed Tomatoes)

Flavor's terrific! Serve with fried chicken, broiled steak or chops, or a roast—

4 medium ripe tomatoes
1 slice Italian or French bread
2 tablespoons snipped parsley
1 small clove garlic, crushed
½ teaspoon crushed oregano
½ teaspoon crushed thyme
¼ teaspoon crushed basil
Dash nutmeg

• • •

½ pound ground veal
2 tablespoons salad oil
2 tablespoons grated Parmesan cheese
1 teaspoon salt
Dash pepper
½ cup soft bread crumbs
1 tablespoon butter or margarine, melted

Cut a slice off top of each tomato and scoop out centers. Invert tomatoes to drain. Soak bread slice in 2 tablespoons water; crumble and combine with parsley, garlic, oregano, thyme, basil, and nutmeg. Brown veal in hot oil; add to herbed mixture. Stir in cheese, salt, and pepper. Spoon filling into tomatoes. Mix bread crumbs and butter; sprinkle over filling. Bake in shallow baking dish in moderate oven (375°) about 20 to 25 minutes. Makes 4 servings.

GRILLED TOMATOES

Great with a steak sandwich—

4 medium ripe tomatoes
½ cup soft bread crumbs
¼ cup shredded sharp process American cheese
2 tablespoons butter or margarine, melted
2 tablespoons snipped parsley

Halve tomatoes (or cut in thick slices). Sprinkle with salt and freshly ground pepper. Mix bread crumbs, cheese, and butter; sprinkle over tomatoes. Trim with snipped parsley. Heat tomatoes, cut side up, on griddle about 5 minutes or till hot through.

turnips

No gardener would ever confuse the turnip and the rutabaga, two edible root members of the mustard family. At the market, turnips are easily recognized by their white skin and purple collar at the base of the leaves. The most often planted variety name describes them well, "Purple Topped White Globe." Rutabagas, often called Swedish turnips, sport a bronze jacket and their deep yellow flesh tends to have the stronger flavor. The commonest market variety name is also descriptive: "Golden Ball."

Buying tips apply to both vegetables: look for smooth skins, firm flesh, and heavy weight for the size. The coating of paraffin improves keeping qualities, preserves their freshness, and flakes off easily when the vegetable is pared. Stored in a cool, dry place, preferably in the refrigerator, turnips and rutabagas will keep well.

In many areas, succulent turnip greens are popular served as a potherb. Select young tops turgid with moisture and fresh green in color.

A fellow root vegetable, the parsnip, lends a sweetness like a dash of sugar when added to stews and soups. For top-quality parsnips, choose small to medium size, firm, and well-shaped vegetables. When parsnips are stored at near-freezing temperatures the sweet-eating quality improves, as starch changes to sugar.

RUTABAGA WHIP

- 3 cups pared and cubed rutabaga
- 3 cups pared and cubed potato
- 2 tablespoons chopped onion
- Light cream
- Butter or margarine
- Salt and pepper

Cook rutabaga, potatoes, and onion in boiling salted water till tender, about 20 minutes. Drain and mash with cream and butter till light and fluffy. Season to taste with salt and pepper. Makes 4 to 6 servings.

LEMON TURNIPS

- 2 cups turnip sticks
- 1 tablespoon butter or margarine
- 2 teaspoons snipped parsley
- 1 teaspoon finely chopped onion
- 1 teaspoon lemon juice

Cook turnip sticks in boiling salted water till just tender, about 20 minutes; drain. Add remaining ingredients. Toss to coat. Serves 4.

RED DOT TURNIPS

- 1 pound turnips, pared and diced
- 2 tablespoons butter or margarine, melted
- 2 teaspoons lemon juice
- 1 tablespoon snipped parsley
- 1 tablespoon chopped canned pimiento

Cook turnips in small amount of boiling salted water till tender; about 12 minutes; drain. Combine remaining ingredients; toss lightly with turnips. Makes 5 servings.

WHIPPED TURNIP PUFF

- 2 cups turnips, cooked and mashed
- 3/4 cup soft bread crumbs
- 3 tablespoons butter or margarine, melted
- 1 tablespoon sugar
- 1 teaspoon salt
- Dash pepper
- 2 slightly beaten eggs

Mix all ingredients together well. Turn into greased 1-quart casserole. Bake at 375° for 40 minutes. Makes 6 servings.

RUTABAGA AND APPLE

3 cups pared rutabaga slices
1 medium apple, thinly sliced
6 tablespoons brown sugar
2 tablespoons butter or margarine

Cook rutabaga slices in boiling salted water till just tender; drain. Place *half* the rutabaga slices in a greased 1-quart casserole along with *half* the apple slices. Sprinkle with *half* the brown sugar; dot with *half* the butter; sprinkle with salt. Repeat layers using remaining ingredients. Bake covered in moderate oven (350°) for 30 minutes. Makes 4 to 6 servings.

VEGETABLE MEDLEY

3 medium turnips pared and diced
1 10-ounce package frozen mixed peas and carrots
2 tablespoons butter or margarine

Cook turnips covered in small amount boiling salted water till tender, 15 to 20 minutes. Cook peas and carrots according to package directions. Drain vegetables and combine. Add butter and season to taste. Serves 6.

TURNIP GREENS SUPREME

Cook one 10-ounce package frozen chopped turnip greens according to package directions; drain thoroughly. Or, remove coarse stems from ½ pound fresh turnip greens; cut in 1-inch pieces. Cook covered in small amount boiling salted water till tender, about 15 minutes. Add torn turnip leaves; cook till tender, 5 minutes longer; drain.

Fry 2 slices bacon until crisp; remove from pan. Blend 1½ tablespoons all-purpose flour into drippings. Add ¾ cup hot water; cook and stir until mixture thickens and boils. Stir in 1 tablespoon sugar, 1½ teaspoons cider vinegar, ½ teaspoon salt, and dash pepper. Add greens; mix and heat through. Garnish with crumbled bacon. Serves 3 or 4.

TURNIPS WITH CHEESE

Cook 3½ cups pared, sliced turnips in boiling salted water till tender, 15 minutes; drain. Meanwhile, melt 2 tablespoons butter in saucepan; blend in 2 tablespoons all-purpose flour, ½ teaspoon salt, and dash pepper. Add 1½ cups milk; cook, stirring constantly, till mixture thickens and bubbles.

Combine sauce and turnips; pour into 1½-quart casserole. Top with ½ cup shredded process cheese. Bake in moderate oven (350°) for 15 to 20 minutes. Serves 6.

EXTRA-SPECIAL PARSNIPS

12 medium parsnips, pared
1 cup crushed pineapple, undrained
½ cup orange juice
½ teaspoon salt
½ teaspoon grated orange peel
2 tablespoons brown sugar
2 tablespoons butter or margarine

Cook parsnips covered in small amount boiling salted water till tender, 25 to 30 minutes; drain. Split lengthwise; place in 10x6x1½-inch baking dish. Combine next 5 ingredients; pour over parsnips. Dot with butter; bake in moderate oven (350°) for 30 to 35 minutes, basting occasionally. Serves 6.

sauces and seasonings

Legends about food and food preparation grow and age and are finally accepted as truths. There's a legend that a saucier must be born, but we swear that she can be made. Patience and industry, a liberal pinch of devotion, and the help of the right pans and whisks, can earn a reputation as a sauce maker for anyone. Proficiency in the use of these several sauces and seasonings will enable you to appreciate a distinctive dish—one with emphatic flavor, a definite contrast, a gourmet's acceptance.

A smidgen of thyme, a flurry of dill, or a pinch of basil can elevate a recipe from mere run of the mill to one that becomes a specialty of the house. The lowly navy bean, laced with the flavor of ginger, produces an aroma that has given it a national reputation. Tomato sauces gently simmering off whiffs of oregano make you watch the clock for time to be called by the dinner bell. These amiable blends of spices and herbs harmonize subtly with crisp cooked vegetables. Just remember this note, seasonings should never shout; they must only sing softly.

WHITE SAUCE

***Medium:* (*Makes 1 cup*)**
- **2 tablespoons butter**
- **2 tablespoons all-purpose flour**
- **1/4 teaspoon salt**
- **1 cup milk**

***Thick:* (*Makes 1 cup*)**
- **3 tablespoons butter**
- **4 tablespoons all-purpose flour**
- **1/4 teaspoon salt**
- **1 cup milk**

***Thin:* (*Makes 1 1/2 cups*)**
- **1 tablespoon butter**
- **1 tablespoon all-purpose flour**
- **1/4 teaspoon salt**
- **1 1/2 cups milk**

For smooth, perfect white sauce, follow these three simple steps. Melt butter or margarine in saucepan over low heat. Blend in flour, salt, and *dash white pepper*, if desired. (See ingredients at upper left.)

Add milk all at once. Cook quickly, stirring constantly, till mixture thickens and bubbles. Make *Medium* White Sauce for sauces, scalloped dishes; *Thin*, for soups, creamed vegetables; *Thick*, for souffles.

Remove sauce from heat when it bubbles. If sauce cooks too long, it becomes too thick and the butter separates out. To repair: Add more milk and cook quickly, stirring constantly, till sauce bubbles.

VELOUTE SAUCE

In a saucepan, melt 2 tablespoons butter or margarine; blend in 3 tablespoons all-purpose flour. Add 1 cup chicken broth and 1/3 cup light cream all at once. Cook quickly, stirring constantly, till mixture thickens and bubbles. Makes 1 1/2 cups.

BECHAMEL SAUCE

Melt 2 tablespoons butter in saucepan. Add 1/4 cup finely chopped onion; cook till soft. Blend in 2 tablespoons all-purpose flour and 1/4 teaspoon salt. Add 1 1/2 cups milk all at once. Cook quickly, stirring constantly, till mixture thickens. Makes 1 1/2 cups.

CLASSIC HOLLANDAISE SAUCE

4 egg yolks
¼ pound (½ cup) butter or margarine, divided in thirds

• • •

2 to 3 teaspoons lemon juice
Dash white pepper
Dash salt

In top of double boiler, place egg yolks and *one-third* of the butter. Over hot, *not boiling*, water, stir rapidly with wooden spoon till butter melts. Add second piece of butter; continue stirring. As mixture thickens and butter melts, add third piece, stirring constantly. (Water in bottom of double boiler should not boil.)

When all butter is melted, remove pan from hot water; stir rapidly 2 minutes longer. Stir in lemon juice, a teaspoon at a time; add seasonings. Again place sauce over hot water, beating constantly till thickened, approximately 2 to 3 minutes.

Remove from heat at once. If sauce should curdle, immediately beat in 1 to 2 tablespoons boiling water. Makes about 1 cup.

SAUCE MOUSSELINE

Into 1 cup cooled Classic Hollandaise, fold ½ cup whipping cream, whipped. Spoon over hot vegetable. Broil about 2 inches from heat a few seconds or till light brown and bubbly. Serve immediately.

JIFFY HOLLANDAISE

Combine ¼ cup salad dressing or mayonnaise and ¼ cup dairy sour cream. Add ½ teaspoon prepared mustard and 1 teaspoon lemon juice. Warm over low heat, stirring constantly, till heated through. (Do not boil.) Makes about ½ cup.

MOCK HOLLANDAISE SAUCE

Blend one 3-ounce package cream cheese, softened, and 2 tablespoons milk. Add 1 egg yolk; blend thoroughly. Add 1½ teaspoons lemon juice and dash salt; beat well. Cook over low heat, stirring constantly, till of a nice sauce consistency. Makes ½ cup.

Classic Hollandaise is a cook's triumph! The proper use of a double boiler will insure your success with this sauce. Notice the top part of the double boiler does not touch the water in the bottom part. Keep the water just below the boiling point for even heat.

BLENDER HOLLANDAISE

3 egg yolks
2 tablespoons lemon juice
Dash cayenne
¼ pound (½ cup) butter or margarine

In blender, place egg yolks, lemon juice, and cayenne. Cover; quickly turn blender on and off. Heat butter till melted and almost boiling. Turn blender on high speed; slowly pour butter into egg mixture, blending till thick and fluffy (about 30 seconds).

Place sauce over warm, not hot, water until serving time. Makes about ⅔ cup.

Crisp-cooked asparagus nestles under creamy, rich Bearnaise Sauce. This classic topping adds an elegant flair to party vegetables. The smooth, subtle flavor complements green beans, broccoli, cauliflower, and artichokes superbly. Garnish with egg slices and serve on a hollow platter filled with hot water to keep the vegetable warm.

BEARNAISE SAUCE

In small saucepan, combine 3 tablespoons tarragon vinegar, 1 teaspoon finely chopped shallots *or* green onion, 4 peppercorns, crushed, and a Bouquet Garni made of a few tarragon and chervil leaves. Simmer till liquid is reduced by half. Strain; add 1 tablespoon cold water to herb liquid.

Beat 4 egg yolks in top of double boiler (not over water). Slowly add herb liquid. Have ½ cup butter or margarine at room temperature. Add a few tablespoons butter or margarine to egg yolks; place over *hot, not boiling,* water. Cook and stir till butter melts and sauce starts to thicken. Continue adding butter and stirring till ½ cup has been used and sauce is smooth as thick cream. Remove from heat. Add salt to taste and 1 teaspoon finely chopped fresh tarragon leaves *or* ¼ teaspoon dried tarragon, crushed. Makes 1 cup sauce.

SAUTERNE SAUCE

¼ cup sauterne
1 tablespoon instant minced onion
¾ cup mayonnaise
2 tablespoons snipped parsley
1 tablespoon lemon juice

In top of double boiler, combine sauterne and onion; let stand 10 minutes. Add remaining ingredients. Heat over hot, *not boiling* water. Makes 1 cup.

SOUR CREAM SAUCE

Combine ½ cup dairy sour cream, 2 tablespoons salad dressing, 2 teaspoons chopped green onion, 1½ teaspoons lemon juice, ½ teaspoon sugar, ¼ teaspoon dry mustard, and dash salt. Heat, stirring constantly, till warm. Makes about ½ cup.

CHEDDAR CHEESE SAUCES

Combine one 10½-ounce can condensed cream of mushroom soup and ⅓ cup milk; heat. Add 1 cup shredded sharp process cheese; stir to melt. Makes 1⅔ cups.

Melt 2 cups shredded sharp process cheese over hot water. Slowly stir in ⅓ cup milk.

To 1 cup hot Medium White Sauce, add 1 cup shredded sharp Cheddar cheese. Stir till melted. Makes 1½ cups sauce.

MORNAY SAUCE

Accented by mellow Gruyere cheese—

2 tablespoons butter or margarine
2 tablespoons all-purpose flour
¼ teaspoon salt
Dash white pepper
1½ cups milk
½ cup diced Gruyere cheese

In saucepan, melt butter; blend in flour, salt, and white pepper. Add milk all at once. Cook quickly, stirring constantly, till mixture thickens and bubbles. Add cheese; stir till melted. Makes 1¾ cups.

SWISS CHEESE SAUCE

½ cup shredded process Swiss cheese
¼ cup mayonnaise or salad dressing
½ cup dairy sour cream

Combine cheese and mayonnaise. Cook over low heat, stirring constantly, till cheese melts. (If necessary, beat smooth with rotary beater.) Mix in sour cream; heat through. Dash with paprika. Serve with hot cauliflower or asparagus. Makes 1 cup.

CREAMY SHRIMP SAUCE

In saucepan, blend ¼ cup chive cream cheese and ¼ cup milk. Add one 10-ounce can frozen condensed cream of shrimp soup. Heat and stir till hot. Add 2 teaspoons lemon juice. Pour over hot cooked broccoli or cauliflower. Sprinkle with 2 tablespoons toasted slivered almonds. Makes 1½ cups sauce.

PARMESAN CHEESE SAUCE

1 tablespoon butter or margarine
1 tablespoon all-purpose flour
¼ teaspoon salt
Dash pepper
Dash paprika
Dash dry mustard
1 cup milk
2 tablespoons grated Parmesan cheese
2 tablespoons toasted slivered almonds

In a saucepan, melt butter; stir in flour, salt, pepper, paprika, and dry mustard. Add milk all at once. Cook and stir till sauce thickens and bubbles. Add cheese and almonds; stir till cheese melts. Makes 1 cup.

BLUE CHEESE SAUCE

Sour cream and blue cheese team up for a rich, tangy treat—

2 tablespoons butter or margarine
2 tablespoons all-purpose flour
1 chicken bouillon cube
1 cup milk
¼ cup dairy sour cream
¼ cup crumbled blue cheese

In a saucepan, melt butter; blend in flour. Add bouillon cube and milk all at once. Cook, stirring constantly, till mixture thickens and bubbles. Remove from heat; stir in sour cream and blue cheese. Heat through, *but do not boil.* Serve with baked potatoes or green vegetables. Makes 1¼ cups.

CREOLE SAUCE

3 tablespoons finely chopped onion
3 tablespoons finely chopped green pepper
1 8-ounce can (1 cup) tomato sauce
1 3-ounce can (⅔ cup) broiled sliced mushrooms, drained
½ teaspoon salt
Dash pepper

Cook onion and green pepper in butter till just tender. Add remaining ingredients; simmer 10 minutes. Makes about 1 cup sauce.

LEMON-BUTTER SAUCE

A quick, all-purpose sauce that adds extra zing to any vegetable—

1/4 cup butter or margarine
1 tablespoon lemon juice
1 tablespoon snipped parsley

Melt butter or margarine in saucepan. Add lemon juice and parsley. Heat a minute or two, until flavors blend. Serve over cooked vegetables. Makes about 1/3 cup sauce.

GOLDENROD SAUCE

1 10 1/2-ounce can condensed cream of celery soup
1/4 cup milk
Dash bottled hot pepper sauce
1 hard-cooked egg

Combine soup, milk, and pepper sauce. Heat thoroughly, stirring occasionally. Pour over hot drained vegetable in serving bowl. Separate egg white and yolk. Chop white and sprinkle around edge of bowl; sieve the yolk over center. Makes 1 1/2 cups.

HORSERADISH SAUCE

1 cup dairy sour cream
3 tablespoons drained prepared horseradish
1/4 teaspoon salt
Dash paprika

Combine all ingredients; mix well. Gently stir into hot, cooked Brussels sprouts, cabbage, or other vegetable. Heat through until vegetables are coated. Makes 1 1/4 cups.

MUSTARD SAUCE

1 cup dairy sour cream
1/4 cup milk
3 tablespoons dry onion-soup mix
2 tablespoons prepared mustard

Combine ingredients. Heat slowly just to bubbling, stirring occasionally. Serve with green vegetables. Makes 1 1/4 cups sauce.

TANGY TOPPING

1/4 cup mayonnaise or salad dressing
1 tablespoon prepared mustard
1 teaspoon prepared horseradish

Combine mayonnaise, mustard, and horseradish. Spoon over hot cooked green beans or broccoli. Sprinkle with paprika.

DILL SAUCE

2 tablespoons butter or margarine
2 tablespoons all-purpose flour
2 cups chicken broth
2 teaspoons sugar
1 1/2 tablespoons vinegar
2 tablespoons finely snipped dill *or* 1 1/2 teaspoons dried dill weed
1 slightly beaten egg yolk

Melt butter in saucepan. Blend in flour; add broth, sugar, vinegar, and dill. Cook, stirring constantly until mixture thickens. Stir small amount of hot mixture into egg yolk; return to hot mixture. Cook and stir 1 minute. Serve with potatoes, peas, cabbage, or beans. Makes 2 1/4 cups.

CHIVE CREAM SAUCE

1 10 3/4-ounce can condensed cream of vegetable soup
1/2 cup milk
1 to 2 tablespoons snipped chives

Mix soup and milk; add chives. Heat, stirring occasionally. Serve with Brussels sprouts, corn, or potatoes. Makes 1 3/4 cups.

CAPER SAUCE

1/4 cup drained chopped sour pickles
2 tablespoons drained finely chopped capers
1 cup mayonnaise or salad dressing
1 1/2 teaspoons prepared mustard
1 1/2 teaspoons snipped parsley

Dry chopped pickles and capers on paper towels. Add to mayonnaise; stir in mustard and parsley. Combine with hot cooked broccoli and heat through. Makes about 1 1/4 cups.

BACON BUTTER

½ cup (¼ pound) butter or margarine
¾ teaspoon prepared mustard
4 slices bacon, crisply cooked and crumbled

Cream butter until light. Blend in remaining ingredients. Makes about ⅔ cup.

CREOLE BUTTER

½ cup (¼ pound) butter or margarine
⅓ cup canned pimientos, sieved
2 tablespoons finely chopped green pepper
2 tablespoons chopped sweet pickle
½ teaspoon salt

Cream butter till light. Add remaining ingredients; mix well. Makes about 1 cup.

HORSERADISH BUTTER

1 cup (½ pound) butter or margarine
¼ cup prepared horseradish
2 tablespoons finely snipped parsley

Cream butter until light. Blend in horseradish and parsley. Makes 1¼ cups.

BROWNED WINE BUTTER

Heat ½ cup butter or margarine until brown. Stir in ¼ teaspoon salt, dash cayenne, and ½ cup white wine; heat through. Makes 1 cup. Pass with hot vegetables.

WHIPPED ONION BUTTER

¼ cup butter or margarine
1 teaspoon Worcestershire sauce
¼ teaspoon dry mustard
¼ teaspoon coarsely ground pepper
2 tablespoons minced onion
2 tablespoons finely snipped parsley

Combine butter, Worcestershire sauce, dry mustard, and pepper. Cream till fluffy. Stir in onion and parsley. Spoon over hot vegetables. Makes about ⅓ cup.

SEASONING SCENTS

Everyone enjoys a touch of mint mingled with crisp-cooked carrots. Parsley and chives have a corner on potato seasoning. But how about thyme, rosemary, basil, or tarragon?

Get acquainted! Make them transform everyday vegetables into a dancing dish. Let your imagination roam over the seasoning shelf. Fancy the spectacular results!

Where to begin? Glance at the Seasoning Guide in this chapter. Some of the seasonings compatible with each vegetable are listed. Use the chart as a guide while you experiment with various seasonings. Then, when you have the knack of seasoning, branch out on your own with the true spirit of adventure!

HERB BUTTERS

½ cup (¼ pound) butter or margarine
1 tablespoon finely snipped fresh herb *or* ¾ teaspoon dried herb
1 teaspoon lemon juice

Cream butter until fluffy. Crush dried herb with mortar and pestle. Combine herb and lemon juice with butter. Keep herb butter at room temperature for 1 hour to mellow before serving. Extra herb butter may be stored in the refrigerator several days.

PARSLEY BUTTER

Delectable on potatoes—next time try another herb and vegetable combination—

Cream ½ cup butter till light. Blend in 1 tablespoon finely snipped parsley, 1 teaspoon lemon juice, ⅛ teaspoon savory, ⅛ teaspoon salt, and dash pepper. Makes ½ cup.

CROUTONS ESPECIAL

Crunchy croutons dashed with herb make a quick dress-up for any vegetable—

Dice bread—white, whole wheat, or rye—in tiny squares (about ⅛ inch). Brown in a little butter in skillet, or fry in deep hot fat. Season with salt and pepper, garlic salt, curry powder, or any favorite herb (refer to Seasoning Guide for ideas.) Sprinkle generously over hot buttered vegetables.

SEASONING GUIDE

	allspice	basil	bay leaves	caraway seed	cardamom	celery seed	chili powder	chives	cinnamon	cloves	curry powder	dill	ginger
artichoke			✓										
asparagus				✓									
green beans		✓	✓								✓	✓	
lima beans						✓	✓				✓		
baked beans										✓			✓
beets	✓		✓	✓		✓				✓		✓	✓
broccoli				✓									
brussels sprouts				✓									
cabbage	✓	✓		✓		✓						✓	
carrots	✓		✓	✓		✓	✓	✓			✓	✓	✓
cauliflower				✓		✓					✓	✓	
corn						✓	✓	✓			✓		
eggplant	✓	✓	✓				✓						
mushrooms													
onions		✓	✓	✓			✓				✓		✓
peas		✓					✓					✓	
white potatoes		✓	✓	✓		✓		✓				✓	
sweet potatoes	✓				✓				✓	✓			✓
spinach	✓	✓							✓			✓	
winter squash	✓	✓							✓	✓			✓
summer squash		✓	✓										
tomatoes		✓	✓	✓		✓	✓			✓	✓	✓	
turnips	✓			✓		✓						✓	

	mace	marjoram	mint	mustard	nutmeg	oregano	poppy seed	rosemary	sage	savory	sesame seed	tarragon	thyme
artichoke													✓
asparagus				✓	✓						✓	✓	
green beans		✓		✓	✓	✓				✓	✓	✓	✓
lima beans						✓			✓				
baked beans				✓		✓							
beets				✓	✓					✓		✓	✓
broccoli				✓		✓						✓	
brussels sprouts				✓	✓				✓				
cabbage			✓	✓	✓	✓				✓		✓	
carrots	✓	✓	✓		✓		✓			✓		✓	✓
cauliflower	✓			✓	✓			✓		✓		✓	
corn													
eggplant		✓							✓				✓
mushrooms								✓				✓	✓
onions				✓	✓	✓	✓		✓				✓
peas		✓	✓	✓		✓	✓	✓	✓	✓			
white potatoes	✓		✓	✓	✓	✓	✓	✓		✓	✓		✓
sweet potatoes					✓		✓						
spinach	✓	✓			✓	✓		✓			✓		
winter squash					✓								
summer squash	✓	✓		✓				✓					
tomatoes						✓		✓	✓		✓		✓
turnips						✓	✓						

soups and chowders

The most popular soup of any country may likely be the best clue to its national cuisine. In this chapter, a cross section of several universal favorites is offered to you. Steaming hot or chilly cold soup, short-cut method or old standard start-from-stock, here's a selection of delicious soups and chowders to end further search.

Classic methods of long gentle simmering, such as French Onion Soup at left, are the way to some. But in the 20th Century kitchen, there's no longer a need to start from scratch to put rich flavor into a soup. Convenience products are a super highway to many a full-bodied soup.

Here you'll find a sampling of old soup favorites such as Split-pea and Ham-bone Bean (with the new simmer-and-short-soak method for fixing the beans or split peas). Out-of-the-ordinary soups feature broccoli, cucumber, or asparagus blended with seasonings that are subtle while enticing. Aristocratic Vichyssoise and borsch have new versions that take little more than a can opener to prepare. This sampling will be a welcome addition to your cooking repertoire.

FRENCH ONION SOUP

You can have this tasty treat ready in a wink when you start with canned beef broth!—

4 large onions, sliced thin
$1/4$ cup butter or margarine
3 $10\frac{1}{2}$-ounce cans (4 cups) condensed beef broth
1 teaspoon Worcestershire sauce
$1/2$ teaspoon salt
Dash pepper
2 French or hard rolls, sliced and toasted
Grated Parmesan cheese

Cook onions in butter till lightly browned, about 20 minutes. Add beef broth and Worcestershire. Bring to boiling; season with salt and pepper. Sprinkle toast generously with Parmesan cheese. Pour soup into bowls and float toast slices on top.

For a gourmet touch, place toast under broiler for a few seconds, just till cheese is lightly browned. Makes 4 to 6 servings.

Note: For the beef broth, you can substitute 4 cups brown stock; or $1\frac{1}{2}$ tablespoons concentrated meat extract dissolved in 4 cups hot water; or 6 beef bouillon cubes dissolved in 4 cups hot water.

CREAM OF ONION SOUP

Melt $1/4$ cup butter or margarine. Add 4 medium onions, thinly sliced, and $1/4$ teaspoon salt. Cover; cook onions till tender.

Meanwhile, prepare white sauce: Melt 2 tablespoons butter or margarine; blend in 2 tablespoons all-purpose flour, $1/2$ teaspoon salt, and dash white pepper. Add 3 cups milk. Cook quickly, stirring constantly till mixture thickens and bubbles.

Add onion mixture and $1/2$ cup milk; heat through. Season to taste. Makes 6 servings.

SMOKY PEA POTAGE

Prepare 1 envelope smoky green-pea-soup mix according to package directions. When soup comes to boiling add 1 small carrot, coarsely shredded, and 1 cup canned luncheon meat or fully cooked ham in thin julienne strips about 1 inch long. Simmer 10 minutes. Makes 3 or 4 servings.

SPLIT-PEA SOUP

Cover 1 pound ($2\frac{1}{4}$ cups) green split peas with 2 quarts (8 cups) cold water; soak overnight. (*Or,* simmer gently 2 minutes, then soak 1 hour.) Add 1 meaty ham bone ($1\frac{1}{2}$ pounds), $1\frac{1}{2}$ cups sliced onion, 1 teaspoon salt, $1/2$ teaspoon pepper, and $1/4$ teaspoon marjoram. Bring to boiling; cover, reduce heat, and simmer (*don't boil*) $1\frac{1}{2}$ hours. Stir occasionally. Remove bone; cut off meat and dice. Return meat to soup; add 1 cup diced celery and 1 cup diced carrots. Cook slowly, uncovered, 30 to 40 minutes. Sprinkle with salt to taste. Makes 6 to 8 servings.

VEGETABLE-BEEF SOUP

3 pounds beef shank, cut in 1-inch pieces
6 cups water
2 cups tomato juice
$1/3$ cup coarsely chopped onion
1 tablespoon salt
2 teaspoons Worcestershire sauce
$1/4$ teaspoon chili powder
2 bay leaves
1 cup diced celery
1 cup sliced carrots
1 cup diced potatoes
1 cup chopped cabbage

Remove meat from bone; cut in bite-size pieces; brown in hot fat. Add bones and 6 cups water. Stir in tomato juice, onion, and seasonings. Cover and simmer 2 hours.

Add vegetables; cover and simmer 1 hour longer. Remove bones and bay leaves before serving. Makes 8 servings.

BEAN 'N VEGETABLE SOUP

Wash 1 pound (2 cups) dry navy beans. Cover with 6 cups water; soak overnight.

Add 1 meaty ham bone ($1\frac{1}{2}$ pounds), 2 medium onions, sliced, $1\frac{1}{2}$ cups sliced carrots, 2 branches celery, thickly sliced, and two 1-pound cans (4 cups) tomatoes.

Season with 1 teaspoon salt, $1/4$ teaspoon pepper, and 1 teaspoon Worcestershire sauce. Simmer covered 3 to $3\frac{1}{2}$ hours.

Remove bone from soup. Mash vegetables slightly. Cut ham from bone; return to soup. Makes 6 to 8 servings.

CORN CHOWDER

Crisp-cook 5 slices bacon; crumble. Reserve 2 tablespoons fat. Cook 2 cups diced potato and 1 cup onion slices in 1 cup boiling salted water till tender. Do not drain. Stir in one 1-pound can whole kernel corn (and liquid), 1 can cream of mushroom soup, 2 cups milk, 1 teaspoon salt, and dash pepper. Blend 2 tablespoons flour with the reserved fat; add. Cook and stir till thick. Simmer 5 minutes; stir often. Top with bacon. Serves 6 to 8.

EASY VEGETABLE SOUP

Long-cooked flavor in mere minutes—

2 14-ounce cans (3½ cups) condensed clear chicken broth
1 10-ounce package frozen mixed vegetables
⅓ cup catsup
¼ cup packaged precooked rice
2 tablespoons dried celery flakes
1 teaspoon Italian salad dressing mix (dry)
1 tablespoon instant minced onion

In large saucepan combine all ingredients. Bring to a boil; reduce heat and simmer 20 minutes. Makes 6 servings.

SOUP-KETTLE SUPPER

In large saucepan combine 1 can condensed cream of vegetable soup, 1 can condensed cream of chicken soup, and 1 can condensed onion soup. Stir in 1½ cups milk and one 12-ounce can (1½ cups) whole kernel corn. Slice one 4-ounce can Vienna sausage in coins. Add sausage to soup.

Cover and heat slowly, stirring occasionally, just till soup comes to boiling. Ladle into bowls. Makes 6 servings.

BEEF-CORN CHOWDER

Combine 1 can condensed beef noodle soup, ¼ cup chopped green pepper, and 2 tablespoons chopped onion. Simmer, covered, until vegetables are tender. Add one 1-pound can (2 cups) whole kernel corn plus liquid, ½ cup cooked diced potatoes, 2 cups milk, dash white pepper, and dash salt.

Cover and heat slowly *just* to boiling, stirring occasionally. Makes 6 servings.

DOUBLE-CORN CHOWDER

6 slices bacon
½ cup chopped onion
1 envelope green-pea-soup mix
2 cups water
1 cup milk
1 1-pound can cream-style corn
1½ to 2 cups cut fresh or frozen corn
1 teaspoon Worcestershire sauce
½ teaspoon seasoned salt

Fry bacon till crisp; remove bacon. Pour all but 1 tablespoon drippings from skillet and add onion; cook till lightly browned. Stir in remaining ingredients and dash pepper. Simmer uncovered 10 minutes, stirring frequently. Crumble bacon on top. Serves 6.

What a colorful way to begin dinner—Hot Tomato Bouillon, here served in a glamorous green leaf bowl. Floaters are avocado slices; accompaniments, toasted cheese strips and warmed crackers. You'll want to file this recipe under "Lovely for Lunch," too.

HOT TOMATO BOUILLON

Just the right light starter for your next big dinner. Or with hearty sandwiches, it's lunch! Delicious either way—

1 10½-ounce can condensed tomato soup
1 10½-ounce can condensed beef broth
½ soup-can water
Dash garlic powder*
Dash crushed oregano
½ medium avocado, thinly sliced

Combine soups, water, and seasonings. Bring to boiling; simmer 5 minutes. Serve in warmed bowls. Float avocado slices on top. Serve with assorted crackers. Serves 4.

*Another time, substitute ¼ teaspoon prepared horseradish, and dash bottled hot pepper sauce for seasonings given. Instead of avocado slices, float a spoonful of dairy sour cream atop each serving.

CREAM OF TOMATO SOUP

Combine one 1-pound 12-ounce can tomatoes, 2 slices onion, 1 bay leaf, 1 teaspoon sugar, 1 teaspoon salt, and ¼ teaspoon pepper. Simmer mixture for 10 minutes; sieve, forcing tomatoes through sieve.

Make white sauce: Melt 2 tablespoons butter or margarine; blend in 2 tablespoons all-purpose flour. Add 1½ cups milk; cook and stir till mixture thickens.

Just before serving, slowly add hot tomato mixture to hot white sauce, stirring constantly. Do not reheat. Serves 6.

TOMATO-CHEESE SOUP

Combine 1 10½-ounce can condensed tomato soup and 1 soup-can milk; heat just to simmering. Add 1 cup shredded process American cheese; stir till melted.

Dot each serving with butter or margarine and snip parsley over. Makes 3 servings.

HERBED TOMATO BROTH

1 10½-ounce can condensed beef broth
1 can condensed tomato soup
1 soup-can water
¼ teaspoon marjoram
¼ teaspoon thyme
Butter or margarine

Combine soups, water, and herbs. Heat to boiling. Reduce heat and simmer 2 minutes. Ladle into bowls. Dot each serving with butter. Makes 5 or 6 servings.

OLD-TIME POTATO SOUP

Flavor is all that's old-fashioned here! Up-to-the-minute ingredients make it easy—

Packaged dry hash brown potatoes (enough for 4 servings)
3 cups water
1⅓ cups instant non-fat dry milk
1 tablespoon instant minced onion
¼ cup instant-type flour
¾ teaspoon salt
Dash pepper
2 tablespoons butter or margarine
Dash rosemary

Cook potatoes according to package directions, but do not drain. Stir in water, then remaining ingredients. Heat to boiling, stirring. Boil 1 minute. Reduce heat; simmer about 5 minutes. Makes 6 servings.

HUNGARIAN POTATO SOUP

½ cup chopped onion
2 tablespoons butter or margarine
4 medium potatoes, diced
1½ teaspoons salt
¼ cup all-purpose flour
1½ teaspoons paprika
1 cup dairy sour cream
2½ cups milk

Cook onion in butter till tender; add potatoes, salt, and 1 cup water. Cover and cook 15 minutes or till tender. Blend flour, paprika, and sour cream till smooth. Stir into potato mixture. Add milk. Heat to boiling, stirring. Cook 1 minute. Season. Serves 6.

SURPRISE POTATO CHOWDER

Empty 1 envelope chowder-style potato-soup mix into saucepan. Gradually stir in 2¼ cups cold water.

Add one 10-ounce package frozen chopped broccoli, 1 tablespoon instant minced onion, and ¼ teaspoon salt. Bring to a boil, separating broccoli pieces with fork.

Simmer covered 10 minutes. Add ¾ cup milk and heat through. Dot each serving with butter. Makes 5 servings.

GOLDEN SQUASH SOUP

Rich, creamy, and just delicious—

¼ cup chopped onion
2 tablespoons butter or margarine
2 tablespons all-purpose flour
½ teaspoon salt
Dash pepper
Dash nutmeg
2 cups milk
1 cup chicken broth
1 cup cooked mashed winter squash
2 tablespoons snipped parsley

Cook onion in butter till tender but not brown. Blend in flour, salt, pepper, and nutmeg. Stir in remaining ingredients; cook and stir till mixture comes to boiling. Serve at once; garnish with parsley sprigs and a sprinkle of nutmeg. Makes 3 or 4 servings.

CHEESY CAULIFLOWER SOUP

2 tablespoons chopped onion
¼ cup butter or margarine
2 tablespoons all-purpose flour
4 cups milk
1 teaspoon salt
Dash pepper
1 medium head cauliflower, cooked and finely chopped
1 cup shredded sharp process American cheese

Cook onion in butter till tender. Blend in flour. Add milk, seasonings, and cauliflower. Cook till smooth and slightly thick, stirring frequently. Add shredded cheese and stir till melted. Makes 4 to 6 servings.

LENTIL-VEGETABLE SOUP

2 cups lentils
8 cups water
2 slices bacon, diced
½ cup chopped onion
½ cup chopped celery
¼ cup chopped carrots
3 tablespoons snipped parsley
1 clove garlic, minced
2½ teaspoons salt
¼ teaspoon pepper
½ teaspoon oregano, crushed

• • •

1 1-pound can (2 cups) tomatoes
2 tablespoons wine vinegar

Rinse lentils; drain; place in soup kettle. Add remaining ingredients, except tomatoes and vinegar. Cover and simmer 1½ hours. Add tomatoes—break up any large pieces. Add vinegar. Simmer covered 30 minutes longer. Season to taste. Makes 8 to 10 servings.

CREAMY LENTIL SOUP

1 cup lentils
2½ cups water
2 teaspoons salt
¼ teaspoon pepper
1 cup finely chopped onion
1 clove garlic, minced
¼ cup tomato sauce
1 bay leaf

• • •

1½ cups milk

Rinse lentils; drain; place in large saucepan. Add remaining ingredients, except milk. Cover and simmer 1 hour. Remove bay leaf.

Press lentil mixture through sieve or blend smooth in blender. Return pureed mixture to saucepan. Add milk; heat and stir till blended and hot. Season to taste. Serves 5 or 6.

PEAS 'N POTATO SOUP

Combine one 12-ounce package frozen hash brown potatoes, 4 cups water, 2 tablespoons instant minced onion, and 1 beef bouillon cube. Cover; cook till potatoes are tender. Stir in two cans condensed split-pea-with-ham soup; add ½ teaspoon garlic powder, and dash pepper. Simmer 5 minutes. Serves 4.

EMERALD ISLE SOUP

1 envelope cream of leek soup mix
1 10-ounce package frozen chopped broccoli
2 cups water
1 teaspoon dried parsley flakes
2 chicken bouillon cubes
¼ teaspoon Worcestershire sauce
Dash pepper
1 cup light cream

Combine soup mix, broccoli, water, parsley flakes, and bouillon cubes. Heat to boiling. Cover and simmer 10 minutes. Blend smooth in blender. Return to saucepan; stir in seasonings and light cream; heat through. Serve with croutons. Makes 5 or 6 servings.

HAM-BONE BEAN SOUP

The wonderful, old-fashioned favorite—

Thoroughly wash 1 pound (about 2⅓ cups) dry navy beans. Cover with 2 quarts (8 cups) cold water; bring to boiling and boil gently 2 minutes. Remove from heat; cover and let stand 1 hour. Do not drain. (Or, if you prefer, soak beans overnight.)

Add one 1½-pound meaty ham bone, ½ teaspoon salt, 6 whole black peppers, and 1 bay leaf. Cover and heat to boiling; boil gently till beans are tender, about 3 to 3½ hours, adding 1 medium onion, sliced, last half hour of cooking.

Remove ham bone; if desired, mash a few of the beans with potato masher. Cut ham from bone; return meat to soup. Season to taste with salt and pepper. Makes 6 servings.

CREAM OF CELERY SOUP

Cook covered 2 cups chopped celery and leaves, and ⅓ cup chopped onion in 1 cup boiling salted water till tender.

Make white sauce: Melt 2 tablespoons butter or margarine. Blend in 2 tablespoons all-purpose flour, ½ teaspoons salt, and dash white pepper. Add 3 cups milk all at once. Cook quickly, stirring constantly, till mixture thickens and boils.

Add vegetables and cooking water; heat. Season to taste. Dot servings with butter or margarine. Makes 6 servings.

Here's just the ticket to please the men in your family—Golden Cheese Soup with Parsley Dumplings. Fluffy green-flecked dumplings simmer in a cheesy vegetable chowder—you'd best be ready with seconds! Serve a crisp green salad as accompaniment.

GOLDEN CHEESE SOUP

1/3 cup grated carrots
1/3 cup chopped celery
2 tablespoons chopped onion
3 tablespoons butter or margarine
1/4 cup all-purpose flour
2 cups milk
1 14-ounce can chicken broth
1 1/4 cups shredded sharp process American cheese
1 recipe Parsley Dumplings

Cook carrots, celery, and onion till tender in 1 cup boiling salted water. Do not drain.

Melt butter in Dutch oven; blend in flour. Add milk; cook, stirring constantly till thick. Add broth, cheese, and vegetables with liquid. Stir over low heat till cheese melts. Drop Parsley Dumplings by teaspoons into simmering soup. Cover tightly; cook over low heat 20 minutes. Serves 6.

PARSLEY DUMPLINGS

1 cup sifted all-purpose flour
2 teaspoons baking powder
1/4 teaspoon salt
2 tablespoons snipped parsley
1/2 cup milk
2 tablespoons melted shortening

Sift together dry ingredients. Add parsley. Combine milk and melted shortening; add to dry ingredients all at once; stir just till flour is moistened. Cook as directed in Golden Cheese Soup recipe.

PUREE MONGOLE

Combine 1 can tomato soup, 1 can green pea soup, and 1 soup-can milk. Heat and stir till blended and hot. Dot each serving with butter. Makes 3 or 4 servings.

Call it soup or salad, Spanish Gazpacho is about the most refreshing, light meal you can find. Pass Skillet Croutons and extra vegetables for sprinkling over top of soup.

GAZPACHO

1 $10\frac{1}{2}$-ounce can condensed beef broth
$2\frac{1}{2}$ cups tomato juice
3 tablespoons lemon juice
2 tablespoons chopped onion
1 clove garlic, sliced lengthwise
$\frac{1}{4}$ teaspoon hot pepper sauce
$\frac{1}{2}$ teaspoon salt
Dash freshly ground pepper
1 cup finely chopped green pepper
1 cup finely chopped cucumber
1 cup finely chopped tomato

In jar, combine first 8 ingredients (spear garlic on toothpick). Cover; shake well. Refrigerate 4 hours. Remove garlic. Place mixture in freezer about 1 hour, but *do not freeze.* Chill soup dishes to keep soup icy cold.

To serve, divide *chilled* vegetables among soup dishes. Pour soup over. Serves 8 to 10.

SPANISH GAZPACHO

1 cup finely chopped peeled tomato
$\frac{1}{2}$ cup finely chopped celery
$\frac{1}{2}$ cup finely chopped cucumber
$\frac{1}{2}$ cup finely chopped green pepper
$\frac{1}{3}$ cup finely chopped green onions
2 teaspoons snipped parsley
1 small clove garlic, minced
2 to 3 tablespoons wine vinegar
2 tablespoons olive oil
1 teaspoon salt
$\frac{1}{4}$ teaspoon freshly ground pepper
$\frac{1}{2}$ teaspoon Worcestershire sauce
2 to $2\frac{1}{2}$ cups tomato juice

Combine all ingredients in stainless steel or glass bowl. Cover and *chill thoroughly*—at least 4 hours. Serve in chilled bowls with Skillet Croutons. Serves 6 to 8.

SKILLET CROUTONS

Nice to pass with Gazpacho. Remember these too, when you're serving a hot soup—

Melt 2 tablespoons butter or margarine in a small skillet; add 1 clove garlic, crushed. Then add 1 cup bread cubes (white, rye, or whole wheat); toss lightly to coat. Cook and stir till croutons are crisp and golden brown.

BLENDER BORSCH

Serve this shocking-pink soup ice-cold right from the blender—

1 cup dairy sour cream
1 1-pound can (2 cups) diced beets, chilled and drained
1 ½-inch slice lemon, peeled
½ small onion, sliced
½ teaspoon salt
½ teaspoon sugar
• • •
1 cup crushed ice

To blender, add ¾ *cup* of the sour cream, the beets, lemon, onion, salt, and sugar. Cover and blend at high speed about 15 seconds. Scrape down sides of container; add ice. Cover and blend about 10 seconds longer. Serve immediately, topped with dollops of remaining sour cream. Makes 5 servings.

CAN-CAN BORSCH

This continental specialty will impress your dinner guests! It's sparkling red with sour-cream snowcaps—beautiful! What's more, you make it all ahead of time—

1 10½-ounce can condensed beef broth, chilled
1 8- to 8½-ounce can (1 cup) julienne or diced beets, chilled
2 tablespoons lemon juice
Dairy sour cream
Snipped chives

Combine beef broth, canned beets (with liquid), and lemon juice. Serve in chilled bowls. Top each serving with a large dollop of sour cream and a sprinkling of snipped chives. Makes 3 servings.

TOMATO SOUPSHAKE

Creamy-smooth, nice tomato-y taste. Add an egg to turn this shake into a soupnog—

1 10¾-ounce can condensed tomato soup
1 cup light cream
½ teaspoon nutmeg
¼ teaspoon salt
• • •
1 egg (optional)

Combine all ingredients in blender or shaker. Blend or shake till smooth. Chill. (If you prefer a thinner soupshake, add a little milk.) Serve in chilled cups, mugs, or glasses. Sprinkle with nutmeg. Serves 4 or 5.

BEEF-O-MATO BREEZE

1 10½-ounce can condensed beef broth
2 cups tomato juice
½ teaspoon instant minced onion
1 teaspoon Worcestershire sauce
1 tablespoon lemon juice

Combine ingredients; chill thoroughly. Garnish each serving with thin slice of lemon. Makes 3½ cups of soup.

CUCUMBER SOUP

This smoothie has just-right tang. Another plus: you do the fixing, then chill it—

1 to 1½ cups grated or ground pared cucumber*
1 quart buttermilk
1 tablespoon chopped green onion
1 teaspoon salt
¼ cup finely snipped parsley
½ teaspoon monosodium glutamate
Dash pepper

Combine all ingredients. Mix well. Cover and chill thoroughly (about 4 hours). Mix again just before serving in chilled cups. Garnish with slices of cucumber and parsley sprigs. Makes 8 to 10 servings.

*Scoop out and discard seeds before grating or chopping. One medium cucumber will give about ⅔ cup grated or ground pulp.

BLENDER BROCCOLI SOUP

1 10-ounce package frozen chopped broccoli
1½ cups milk
1 cup light cream
2 beef bouillon cubes
1 teaspoon instant minced onion
¼ teaspoon salt
Dash *each* pepper and nutmeg

Partially thaw broccoli; break in small pieces; place in blender with ½ *cup* milk. Blend till broccoli is very fine. Add remaining ingredients. Blend smooth, 45 to 60 seconds. Chill. Top with sour cream. Serves 4 to 6.

CREAMY VICHYSSOISE

3 cups boiling water
2 chicken bouillon cubes
2 tablespoons dry onion-soup mix
2 tablespoons celery flakes
1 tablespoon parsley flakes
Packaged instant mashed potatoes (enough for 4 servings)
1 cup whipping cream
Snipped chives

To boiling water add bouillon cubes, soup mix, celery flakes, and parsley flakes. Cover and simmer 10 minutes; strain.

Stir in mashed potatoes; beat with fork till smooth. Blend in cream and chill thoroughly. Garnish with chives before serving. Makes 4 to 6 servings.

QUICK VICHYSSOISE

1 10-ounce can frozen condensed cream of potato soup
1 10½-ounce can condensed cream of chicken soup
1 soup-can milk
1 cup light cream

Heat potato soup to thaw. Pour into blender or mixer bowl. Add cream of chicken soup and milk. Blend or beat till smooth. Add cream; blend few more seconds. Cover and chill well, 3 or 4 hours or overnight. (If desired, blend again just before serving.) Snip chives over soup. Makes 5 servings.

CLASSIC FRENCH VICHYSSOISE

One of the all-time greats—

4 leeks (white part), thinly sliced
1 medium onion, thinly sliced
¼ cup butter or margarine

• • •

5 medium potatoes, thinly sliced (about 4 cups)
4 cups chicken broth
1 tablespoon salt

• • •

2 cups milk
2 cups light cream
1 cup whipping cream

Cook leeks and onion in butter till tender but not brown. Add potatoes, broth, and salt. Cook 35 to 40 minutes.

Rub mixture through fine sieve; return to heat. Add milk and light cream. Season to taste with salt and pepper. Bring to boiling; cool. Rub through very fine sieve.

When cold, add whipping cream. Chill. Garnish with snipped chives. Serves 8.

CHILLED ASPARAGUS SOUP

No better way to begin a summer luncheon. A flick of the blender switch produces this soup in seconds—

1 10-ounce package frozen cut asparagus
2 cups milk
1 teaspoon instant minced onion
1 teaspoon salt
Dash pepper
½ cup light cream

• • •

Dairy sour cream

Cook asparagus according to package directions; drain well. Combine asparagus with *1 cup* of the milk, the onion, salt, and pepper in a blender. Blend till smooth, about 10 seconds. Add 1 cup milk; blend 5 seconds longer. Add light cream; blend 5 seconds. Chill 3 to 4 hours.

If desired, top each serving with a dollop of sour cream. Makes 4 to 6 servings.

CHILLED TOMATO-CHEESE SOUP

An absolutely delicious meal starter! Be sure to try it—

1 10½-ounce can condensed tomato soup
2 cups light cream
1 teaspoon lemon juice
1 teaspoon prepared horseradish
Few drops bottled hot pepper sauce

• • •

½ cup cream-style cottage cheese
¼ cup chopped green onions
1 teaspoon salt
¼ teaspoon pepper
Dairy sour cream

Combine soup, cream, lemon juice, horseradish, and bottled hot pepper sauce. Beat with electric mixer or rotary beater till well blended. Add cottage cheese, green onions, salt, and pepper; mix well. Chill.

Serve in chilled bowls. If desired, top each serving with a fluff of dairy sour cream. Makes 4 to 6 servings.

JELLIED TOMATO CONSOMME

Refreshing barbecue starter—

1 envelope (1 tablespoon) unflavored gelatin
1 10½-ounce can condensed consomme
1¾ cups tomato juice
½ teaspoon bottled steak sauce
Salt
Pepper
¼ teaspoon paprika
2 honeydew melons, halved
Fresh mint
Lemon wedges

Soften gelatin in ½ *cup* cold consomme in bowl. Heat tomato juice just to boiling; add to gelatin and stir to dissolve. Add remaining consomme and seasonings; chill till firm. Break up gelatin with fork. Spoon into chilled honeydew melon halves.

If desired, trim with sprigs of mint and offer lemon wedges. Makes 4 servings.

SOUP TOPPERS

The crunch or color of an attractive garnish can lift any soup to the "very special" class. Try these ideas on soups that make a light lunch or begin an elegant dinner.

For croutons, toast 2 cups bread cubes in shallow pan in a slow oven (325°), stirring frequently till browned. Sprinkle over hot soup, or store covered in a jar.

Toasted slivered almonds are especially good over potato soup. Buy almonds already slivered. Just spread the nuts on a baking sheet and toast in a slow oven (325°) for about 15 minutes, stirring once or twice.

Some other crunchy toppers include popped corn, crumbled bacon, and potato or corn chips. Try making a raft sometime of your favorite kind of cracker. Top the cracker with a fluff of whipped cheese.

For color, try sprinkling hot or cold soups with snipped parsley or chives, paprika, or sieved hard-cooked egg yolk. Fast color pick-ups can be a sprig of parsley or a slice of hard-cooked egg.

Most cold soups sing with the rich flavor of a dollop of sour cream. Hot soups are grand with a pat of butter.

CHILLED CELERY SOUP

1 10½-ounce can condensed cream of celery soup
2 tablespoons chopped green pepper
1½ cups milk

Combine all ingredients in a blender; cover and blend till smooth. Chill at least 4 hours or served over cracked ice in chilled glasses, cups, or mugs. Garnish with sprigs of fresh mint if desired. Makes 3 or 4 servings.

VEGETABLE COCKTAIL SOUP

Quickest cold soup ever made—

1 10½-ounce can condensed beef broth
1 12-ounce can vegetable-juice cocktail

Combine broth and juice. Serve immediately over cracked ice. Makes 4 or 5 servings.

salads and garnishes

Stop here for spectacular salads, for shimmering molded salads as well as tossed salad-bowl beauties. Above is Tangy Spinach Toss, inspired by the old-fashioned wilted lettuce salad—and maybe even better! The last minute before serving, a hot dressing, lively with lemon and horseradish, is poured over crisp spinach leaves.

And this chapter has more: A collection of dressings, each with just the right zest to complement vegetable salads; zippy relishes—the little extras that make everyday meals extraordinary; gay garnishes to trim a salad.

Take your choice from our fabulous salads. Let these recipe ideas help you star as a hostess on every occasion. Some are perfect for a party . . . others are just right for family night. All of them will bring you praise a-plenty!

TANGY SPINACH TOSS

1/4 cup butter or margarine
2 tablespoons sliced green onion
2 tablespoons all-purpose flour
1/4 teaspoon salt
1 cup water
2 tablespoons lemon juice
1 tablespoon prepared horseradish
1/2 teaspoon Worcestershire sauce
2 hard-cooked eggs
1 pound fresh spinach, torn in bite-size pieces

Cook onion in butter about 1 minute; blend in flour and salt. Add water, lemon juice, horseradish, and Worcestershire; cook and stir till mixture boils. Dice *one* egg; add to dressing. Pour dressing over spinach in salad bowl; toss lightly. Slice remaining egg for garnish; sprinkle with paprika; serve at once. Makes 6 to 8 servings.

GREEN GODDESS SALAD

6 cups torn romaine, chilled, dry, and crisp
3 cups torn curly endive, chilled, dry, and crisp
1 9-ounce package frozen artichoke hearts, cooked, drained, chilled
1/2 cup pitted ripe olives, sliced
1 2-ounce can rolled anchovy fillets
2 medium tomatoes, cut in wedges (if desired)
Creamy Green Goddess Dressing

Combine ingredients (except dressing) in large salad bowl. Top with 1/3 cup dressing; roll-toss several times to coat every leaf. Serve on chilled salad plates. Pass extra dressing. Makes 6 servings.

CREAMY GREEN GODDESS DRESSING

Blend 1 cup mayonnaise with 1/2 cup dairy sour cream. Stir in 1/3 cup snipped parsley, 3 tablespoons finely snipped chives, 3 tablespoons anchovy paste, 3 tablespoons tarragon vinegar, 1 tablespoon lemon juice, and dash freshly ground pepper. Chill thoroughly. Makes 2 cups dressing.

TOSSED WESTERN SALAD

Tossed salad can take little last-minute fussing —here's one to prove it! In the morning, fix greens and marinate artichoke hearts (marinade doubles as dressing). Come dinner time, tossed salad's a snap!—

1 9-ounce package frozen artichoke hearts
1/2 cup salad oil
1/4 cup lemon juice
3 tablespoons tarragon vinegar
2 tablespoons sugar
2 tablespoons minced onion
1 clove garlic, crushed
1 teaspoon salt
1/2 teaspoon dry mustard
Freshly ground pepper

• • •

3 heads Bibb or 2 heads Boston lettuce
2 medium heads romaine lettuce
1/2 bunch radishes
1 avocado
1 cup packaged croutons
2 tablespoons butter or margarine

Cook artichoke hearts according to package directions; drain *well.* Combine oil, lemon juice, vinegar, sugar, and seasonings in jar; cover and shake. Pour dressing over artichokes; cover and chill several hours or overnight, stirring occasionally.

Several hours before serving, wash greens; drain well on a towel. Tear greens in bite-size pieces and layer with paper towels in large bowl or other container; cover with damp towel; refrigerate. (Greens chilled this way are extra crisp.)

Slice radishes; place in bowl; cover and chill. Slice avocado and place in another small bowl. (To hold color of sliced avocado, sprinkle with a little of the dressing from artichokes.) Cover well and chill. In small skillet, brown croutons in butter, stirring till toasted on all sides. (Croutons are best served warm—if fixed ahead, reheat in oven a few minutes.)

To serve salad, fluff crisp dry greens into salad bowl; add chilled artichokes and dressing, and sliced radishes. Roll-toss till every lettuce leaf is coated with dressing. Season with salt and freshly ground pepper. Add avocado and warm croutons; toss gently. Makes about 8 servings.

Iceberg lettuce

Boston lettuce

Bibb lettuce

Water cress

GUACAMOLE BOWL WITH AVOCADO DRESSING

Unusual combination and just delicious—

Line salad bowl with romaine—about ½ head. Break ½ medium head lettuce into bowl. Add 8 to 10 cherry tomatoes, halved, or 2 medium tomatoes, cut in wedges.

Add ½ cup sliced pitted ripe olives, ¼ cup sliced green onions, 1 cup corn chips, and 1 ripe avocado, peeled and sliced.

Toss gently with Avocado Dressing. Top with ½ cup shredded Cheddar cheese. Serve at once. Makes 4 or 5 servings.

AVOCADO DRESSING

1 ripe avocado
1 tablespoon lemon juice
½ cup dairy sour cream
⅓ cup salad oil
1 clove garlic, crushed
½ teaspoon sugar
½ teaspoon chili powder
¼ teaspoon salt
¼ teaspoon bottled hot pepper sauce

Peel avocado; remove seed. With blender or electric mixer, mash avocado. Add remaining ingredients; blend or beat smooth

Romaine

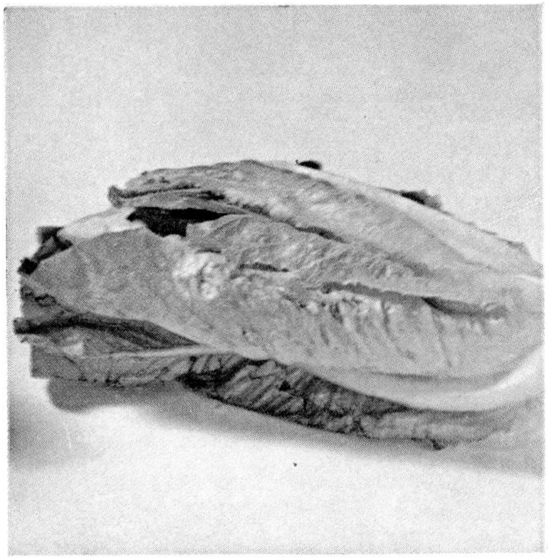

Curly endive

Leaf lettuce

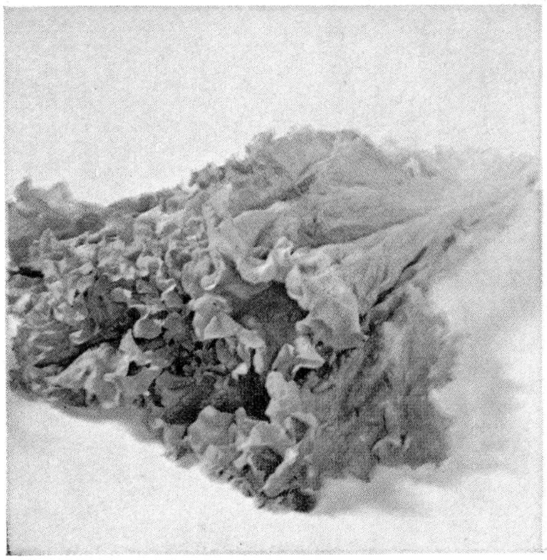

Escarole

SPRING SALAD BOWL

1 bunch leaf lettuce, torn in bite-size pieces
½ bunch water cress
1½ cups tiny spinach leaves
24 carrot curls
4 green onions with tops, chopped
12 pitted ripe olives (optional)
12 blanched almonds, toasted (optional)

Combine greens, carrot curls, and onions. Stuff olives with almonds and add. Toss with Italian dressing. Makes 6 servings.

CALICO COLESLAW

4 cups finely shredded crisp green cabbage
1 12-ounce can (1½ cups) whole kernel corn, drained
½ cup finely chopped onion
¼ cup chopped green pepper
¼ cup chopped canned pimiento
½ teaspoon salt
½ to ¾ cup mayonnaise

Combine first 5 ingredients. Chill thoroughly. Just before serving, add salt and mayonnaise; toss lightly. Serves 6 to 8.

Trick for coring lettuce: Remove any not-so-pretty leaves. Rinse head well under cold water, but don't soak. Smack the head stem end down on counter top. You can twist the core right out!

For lettuce cups, run water through core; drain. Gently peel off leaves. To add a party touch, use two or three lettuce cups and arrange to make one big perfect holder for mound of chicken or sea-food salad.

Refrigerate remainder of head—in crisper, plastic bag, clear plastic wrap, or foil.

Salad baskets are specially designed to remove water from freshly washed greens with as little handling as possible. (The little basket is for parsley.)

Wash greens under cold running water; pile into basket. Swing or shake basket gently to remove water. Salad dressing coats *dry* leaves evenly, but runs off wet leaves.

When greens are safe in the crisper, the big basket collapses for easy storage.

To keep water cress and parsley fresh and green, refrigerate in tightly covered jar.

No wire salad basket? Drain excess water from head lettuce on rack or on paper towels. Toss leafy greens like romaine or escarole in clean kitchen towel or in paper towels.

Fix romaine French-style for tossed salad. On board, cut out rib in each leaf with two strokes of the paring knife.

At salad-tossing time, tear greens into bite-size pieces—don't cut them with a knife or you'll bruise them. They even taste better when torn!

Use enough dressing to coat greens thoroughly. "Easy does it" with the tossing—tender greens deserve the light touch.

Pretty trim for salad bowl: Snip points in romaine leaves with kitchen scissors; stand upright around edge of salad.

ORIGINAL CAESAR SALAD

3 medium heads romaine lettuce, chilled, dry, and crisp
About 1/3 cup Garlic Olive Oil
2 to 3 tablespoons wine vinegar
1 lemon, halved
1 or 2 1-minute coddled eggs
Dash Worcestershire sauce
Salt and freshly ground pepper
1/3 cup grated Parmesan cheese
About 1 cup Caesar Croutons

Break romaine leaves in 2- or 3-inch widths. At *last minute* before serving, place romaine in chilled salad bowl. Drizzle with Garlic Olive Oil, then vinegar. Squeeze lemon over, using fork to help free juice. Break in eggs. Season with Worcestershire and salt. Grind pepper over all. Sprinkle with Parmesan cheese. Roll-toss 6 or 7 times, or till dressing is well combined and every leaf is coated. Add Croutons; toss once or twice. Serve *at once* on chilled dinner plates. Garnish with rolled anchovies, if desired. Makes 6 servings as main course.

Garlic Olive Oil: Prepare one to several days early. Slice 6 cloves of garlic lengthwise in quarters; let stand in 1 cup olive oil (or use salad oil or half of each).

Caesar Croutons: Cut each slice of bread in 5 strips one way, then across 5 times to make squares. Spread out on baking sheet; pour a little Garlic Olive Oil over. Heat at 225° for 2 hours or till very dry. Sprinkle with grated Parmesan cheese. Store in covered jar in refrigerator.

CREAMY POTATO SALAD

Cook 7 medium potatoes in jackets; peel and slice, making 6 cups. While potatoes are warm, pour 1/3 cup clear French or Italian dressing over. Chill 2 hours.

Add 3/4 cup sliced celery and 1/3 cup sliced green onions and tops.

Chop whites of 4 hard-cooked eggs; add. Sieve yolks; reserve some for garnish. Combine remaining sieved yolks with 1 cup mayonnaise, 1/2 cup dairy sour cream, and 1 1/2 teaspoons prepared horseradish mustard. Fold into salad. Add salt and celery seed to taste. Chill 2 hours.

Add 1/3 cup diced pared cucumber. Sprinkle reserved yolk over top. Makes 8 servings.

FRESH VEGETABLE CROWN

Form a crown of the following chilled, cooked fresh vegetables by alternating them on a bed of shaved lettuce: strips of cauliflower, beet slices, carrot slices, peas, green beans, and zucchini slices, rising to a pinnacle of broccoli. For pretty slices of cooked beets and carrots, use a waffle cutter. Snip points on a few crisp romaine leaves and stand them upright around edge of salad. Pass Thousand Island Dressing.

SUNFLOWER SALAD

Combine in bowl 1 1/2 to 2 cups drained, canned or cooked tiny peas, 1 1/2 to 2 cups drained, canned or cooked baby Lima beans, 1/2 cup sliced pitted ripe olives, and 1/4 cup sliced stuffed green olives.

Mix 1/2 cup mayonnaise or salad dressing with 2 tablespoons grated onion, 1 tablespoon lemon juice, 2 teaspoons liquid drained from capers, 1 tablespoon capers, 1/2 teaspoon salt, and dash pepper. Pour over salad; mix gently. Cover; marinate in refrigerator several hours, mixing occasionally.

With vegetable parer, slice 2 or 3 pared medium carrots lengthwise, making thin strips. (Rest carrot on board and pare away from you.) Chill slices in ice water to crisp.

Add 1/4 cup salted peanuts to salad, if desired. Mound salad in center of lettuce-lined plate. Arrange drained carrot strips around salad. Trim with additional ripe olives, if desired. Makes 8 servings.

MEXICAN BEAN SALAD

1 1-pound can (2 cups) cut green beans
1 1-pound can (2 cups) dark red kidney beans
1 1-pound can (2 cups) chick peas or garbanzo beans
1 cup garlic French dressing
Crisp salad greens

Drain beans and peas. Toss with dressing. Chill several hours or overnight, stirring a few times. Just before serving, stir again; drain off excess dressing. Spoon salad onto lettuce-lined plates. Sprinkle with sweet pickle relish, if desired. Makes 10 servings.

GARDEN SALAD BOWL

This is the beauty pictured at left—

1 small head lettuce
2 pounds fresh *or* 2 10-ounce packages frozen asparagus, cooked, drained, and chilled
2 tomatoes, cut in wedges
1 cucumber, sliced
2 hard-cooked eggs, sliced
½ cup sliced pitted ripe olives

Have salad ingredients chilled thoroughly. Tear lettuce in bite-size pieces in salad bowl. Arrange asparagus spears in spokes with tips at outer edge of bowl. Place tomato wedges and cucumber slices between spokes. Place egg slices in center, top with olive slices. Serve with a tangy French dressing. Makes 8 servings.

ITALIAN SALAD PLATTER

¼ cup sauterne
1 envelope Italian salad-dressing mix
½ cup salad oil or olive oil
¼ cup white wine vinegar
¼ cup finely sliced green onions
3 tablespoons drained sweet-pickle relish
2 tablespoons snipped parsley
2 tablespoons finely chopped green pepper
5 or 6 medium zucchini squash
3 or 4 medium tomatoes, chilled
Pink Onions

Pour sauterne into a jar. Add dressing mix; cover; shake. Add next 6 ingredients.

Slice each zucchini in 6 lengthwise strips. Cook in boiling salted water until *just* tender, 3 to 5 minutes. Drain; arrange in shallow dish. Shake dressing; pour over. Cover; refrigerate several hours or overnight; spoon dressing over zucchini occasionally.

To serve, slice tomatoes; drain zucchini and arrange on lettuce-lined platter with tomatoes. Center with Pink Onions. Makes 8 or 9 servings.

Pink Onions: Cut 1 large onion in ¼-inch slices; separate in rings; marinate several hours in liquid from pickled beets. Drain; toss with a few white onion rings.

CONFETTI ASPARAGUS TOSS

1 pound fresh asparagus, cut in 2-inch pieces (2 cups)
1 small head lettuce, torn in bite-size pieces (4 cups)
1 cup sliced celery
¼ cup sliced green onions and tops
½ cup salad oil
2 tablespoons white wine vinegar
2 tablespoons lemon juice
¼ cup finely chopped cooked beets
1 hard-cooked egg, finely chopped
1 tablespoon snipped parsley
1 teaspoon paprika
1 teaspoon sugar
1 teaspoon salt
½ teaspoon dry mustard
4 drops bottled hot pepper sauce

Cook asparagus till just tender; drain. Chill. Combine with lettuce, celery, and onion. For dressing*, combine remaining ingredients in jar; cover and shake well. Pour dressing over salad; toss lightly till well coated. Makes 6 to 8 servings.

*If desired, use one envelope French salad-dressing mix and omit last 5 ingredients listed above.

CAULIFLOWER-CHEESE TOSS

¼ cup olive oil
¼ cup salad oil
¼ cup white wine vinegar
1 teaspoon salt *and* dash pepper
1 medium onion, thinly sliced and separated in rings
½ small head cauliflower, sliced (about 3 cups)
½ cup sliced radishes
Romaine leaves
1 medium head Iceberg lettuce, torn in bite-size pieces (about 8 cups)
½ cup crumbled blue cheese

Combine olive oil, salad oil, vinegar, salt, and pepper. Add onion, cauliflower, and radishes to mixture. Marinate for at least 30 minutes. Line salad bowl with romaine leaves; add Iceberg lettuce; sprinkle crumbled cheese over lettuce. Just before serving, add marinade mixture and toss gently with lettuce and blue cheese. Makes 6 servings.

TOMATO RELISH SALAD

3 medium tomatoes, sliced
1 cup thinly sliced unpared cucumber
1 medium onion, thinly sliced
1/2 cup thinly sliced carrot rounds
1/2 cup thinly sliced celery
1/2 cup tarragon vinegar
1/3 cup water
1/4 cup sugar
1 teaspoon paprika
1 teaspoon basil leaves, crushed
1/2 teaspoon salt
1/4 teaspoon freshly ground pepper

Arrange tomato slices, cucumber, onion, carrots, and celery in rows in 10x6x1 1/2-inch baking dish. Combine remaining ingredients; pour over vegetables. Cover; chill at least 4 hours or overnight, turning vegetables occasionally. Makes 6 to 8 servings.

SALADE NICOISE

In large salad bowl combine one 1-pound can (2 cups) whole green beans, drained; one 15-ounce can (1 1/2 cups) artichoke hearts, drained and quartered; one 6 1/2- or 7-ounce can tuna, flaked; one 7 1/2-ounce can pitted ripe olives, sliced; one 4-ounce jar pimientos, drained and sliced; and one 2-ounce can flat fillet of anchovies, drained.

Add 1/4 cup Italian dressing; toss lightly. Chill thoroughly. Just before serving, toss again. Makes 6 to 8 servings.

ITALIAN SALAD BOWL

1/2 medium head lettuce, torn in bite-size pieces
1/2 medium head romaine, torn in bite-size pieces
2 cups thinly sliced raw zucchini
1/2 cup sliced radishes
1/2 cup sliced fresh mushrooms
3 green onions, sliced
Salt and pepper
Italian or wine-vinegar dressing
1/2 cup crumbled blue cheese

In large bowl, combine first 6 ingredients. Season to taste with salt and pepper. Toss lightly with dressing; sprinkle crumbled blue cheese over top. Makes 6 servings.

SARAH'S SALAD

A most unusual salad! It chills several hours to mellow and make its own dressing—

2 cups torn head lettuce
2 cups torn curly endive
2 cups torn romaine lettuce
6 tablespoons mayonnaise
1 medium red or white onion, thinly sliced
1 1/2 cups drained cooked peas
1 cup julienne strips natural Swiss cheese
6 slices bacon, crisp-cooked

Place a *third* of the salad greens in a bowl; dot with several tablespoons of the mayonnaise. Top with a *third* of the onion slices; sprinkle with sugar (about 1 teaspoon). Dash with salt (about 1/4 teaspoon) and freshly ground pepper. Add a *third* of the peas and cheese. Repeat layers, seasoning each. *Do not toss.* Cover; chill 2 hours.

Just before serving, crumble bacon over top and toss. Makes 6 servings.

TAOS SALAD TOSS

2 cups chopped lettuce
1 1-pound can (2 cups) dark red kidney beans, drained
2 medium tomatoes, chopped and drained
1 tablespoon chopped, canned green chiles
1 medium avocado, mashed
1/2 cup dairy sour cream
2 tablespoons Italian dressing
1 teaspoon chili powder
1 teaspoon instant minced onion
1/4 teaspoon salt
Dash pepper
1/2 cup shredded sharp Cheddar cheese
1/2 cup crushed corn chips

Combine lettuce, kidney beans, tomatoes, and green chiles in salad bowl; chill thoroughly. Blend avocado and sour cream. Add next 5 ingredients; mix well; chill.

Season salad with salt and pepper. Toss with avocado dressing. Top with cheese and corn chips. Garnish with ripe olives, if desired. Makes 4 to 6 servings.

FRENCH DRESSING

Classic clear French—piquant, pretty—

½ cup salad oil
2 tablespoons vinegar
2 tablespoons lemon juice
1 teaspoon sugar
½ teaspoon salt
½ teaspoon dry mustard
½ teaspoon paprika
Dash cayenne

Put ingredients in jar; cover and shake well before using. Makes ¾ cup.

Blue-cheese French Dressing: Add 2 ounces blue cheese, crumbled, to recipe above.

VINAIGRETTE DRESSING

1 cup clear French dressing
2 tablespoons chopped stuffed green olives
1 tablespoon chopped canned pimiento
1 tablespoon snipped chives
1 hard-cooked egg, chopped

Combine ingredients in jar; cover and shake vigorously until well mixed. Makes about 1¼ cups. Nice with spinach salad or greens.

BLUE-CHEESE DRESSING

Soften one 3-ounce package cream cheese. Blend in ½ cup crumbled blue cheese. Slowly add ½ cup mayonnaise, ½ cup light cream, and 1 tablespoon lemon juice. Beat smooth. Chill. Makes about 2 cups.

ITALIAN DRESSING

1 cup salad oil
¼ cup vinegar
1 teaspoon salt
½ teaspoon white pepper
½ teaspoon celery salt
¼ teaspoon cayenne
¼ teaspoon dry mustard
1 clove garlic, minced
Dash bottled hot pepper sauce

Combine ingredients in jar; cover and shake.

TANGY FRENCH DRESSING

⅔ cup salad oil
⅔ cup vinegar
⅓ cup water
2 tablespoons snipped chives or green onion
2 teaspoons sugar
1 teaspoon paprika
2 teaspoons Worcestershire sauce
½ teaspoon salt
½ teaspoon celery salt
¼ teaspoon dry mustard
Dash pepper

Combine ingredients; shake well in covered jar. Makes 1¾ cups. Serve over greens.

THOUSAND ISLAND DRESSING

To 1 cup mayonnaise or salad dressing, add ¼ cup chili sauce; 2 hard-cooked eggs, chopped or sieved; 2 tablespoons chopped green pepper; 2 tablespoons chopped celery; 1½ tablespoons finely chopped onion; 1 teaspoon paprika; and ½ teaspoon salt. Mix well. Makes 1½ cups dressing.

LOW-CALORIE DRESSING

In jar, combine one 8-ounce can tomato sauce, 2 tablespoons tarragon vinegar, 1 teaspoon onion juice, 1 teaspoon Worcestershire sauce, and ½ teaspoon *each* salt, dill seed, and basil. Shake well. Chill. Calories per tablespoon: 5.

SOUR-CREAM SPECIAL

1 cup dairy sour cream
½ cup finely chopped, well-drained cucumber
¼ cup finely chopped green onions
¼ cup finely chopped radishes
1 tablespoon tarragon vinegar
1 to 1½ teaspoons prepared horseradish
¾ teaspoon salt

Combine ingredients; chill. Makes about 1⅓ cups. Use as a dip for cucumber and celery sticks, or dressing for lettuce wedges. Top with extra horseradish, if desired.

PICKLED ONION RINGS

1 cup water
1 cup white vinegar
¼ cup sugar
½ teaspoon salt
6 inches stick cinnamon, broken in pieces
2 teaspoons whole cloves
10 drops red food coloring
1 large sweet onion, thinly sliced and separated in rings (about 4 cups)

Combine first 6 ingredients; simmer, covered, 10 minutes; strain. Add food coloring; pour hot mixture over onions. Chill at least 4 hours; turn occasionally. Drain.

PICKLED CARROTS

Scrape 6 medium carrots (about 1 pound) and cut in 3-inch lengths. Precook 5 minutes. Drain; cut in thin sticks.

Combine ¾ cup sugar, ¾ cup vinegar, ¾ cup water, and 1 tablespoon mustard seed. In cloth bag tie 2½ inches stick cinnamon, broken, and 3 whole cloves; add to sugar-water mixture. Simmer 10 minutes; pour over carrots; cool. Refrigerate 8 hours or overnight. Drain well before serving.

SALSA

A traditional Mexican-style sauce that's a must in peak tomato season. Serve as relish with meats, omelets—

4 medium firm, ripe tomatoes, peeled and finely chopped
½ cup finely chopped onion
½ cup finely chopped celery
¼ cup finely chopped green pepper
¼ cup olive oil or salad oil
2 tablespoons red wine vinegar
1 tablespoon mustard seed
1 teaspoon coriander seed, crushed
2 to 3 tablespoons drained canned finely chopped green chiles
1 teaspoon salt
Dash pepper

Mix all ingredients. Chill several hours or overnight. Makes 3 cups.

MUSTARD BEANS

Combine 1 cup sugar, ½ cup cider vinegar, 3 tablespoons prepared mustard, ½ teaspoon instant minced onion, and ¼ teaspoon salt. Bring to boiling, stirring to dissolve sugar. Add one 1-pound can yellow wax beans, drained. Simmer uncovered 5 minutes; cool. Cover; refrigerate overnight.

SVENGALI TOMATOES

1 1-pound can (2 cups) tomatoes cut up
¼ cup cranberry-orange relish
2 tablespoons raisins
1 tablespoon sugar
½ teaspoon salt
½ teaspoon ginger
¼ teaspoon cayenne

Combine all ingredients in saucepan; simmer 8 to 10 minutes. Serve warm or chilled.

ZIPPY BEET SALAD

Soften 1 envelope (1 tablespoon) unflavored gelatin in ½ cup cold water; heat and stir over low heat till gelatin dissolves.

To ⅔ cup pickled-beet liquid, add water to make 1½ cups; add to gelatin along with ½ teaspoon salt and ¼ teaspoon grated onion. Chill till partially set. Stir in 1 cup chopped pickled beets and 1 cup finely shredded cabbage. Turn into 3-cup mold; chill till firm. Unmold on greens. Serves 6.

CREAMY BROCCOLI MOLD

Soften 1 envelope unflavored gelatin in ¾ cup cold water. Cook one 10-ounce package frozen chopped broccoli as directed on package, adding 2 chicken bouillon cubes, 1 tablespoon instant minced onion, and 1 teaspoon monosodium glutamate. *Do not add salt. Do not drain.* Add softened gelatin; stir to dissolve. Combine broccoli mixture with ½ cup dairy sour cream, ½ cup chopped celery, ¼ cup chopped canned pimiento, 2 tablespoons snipped parsley, and 2 tablespoons lemon juice. Chill until partially set. Pour into 5½-cup ring mold; chill till firm. Unmold on lettuce-lined plate. Makes 6 to 8 servings.

Old-fashioned Perfection Salad has been a winner at the dinner table for generations. And no wonder! It's perfect with baked ham, a pot roast—almost any meat. It's tang and crunch and pretty calico colors come to the rescue for distinguished meals.

PERFECTION SALAD

In a mixing bowl, thoroughly combine 2 envelopes (2 tablespoons) unflavored gelatin, ½ cup sugar, and 1 teaspoon salt. Add 1½ cups boiling water and stir to dissolve gelatin. Then add 1½ cups cold water, ½ cup vinegar, and 2 tablespoons lemon juice. Chill till mixture is partially set.

Add 2 cups finely shredded cabbage, 1 cup chopped celery, ¼ cup chopped green pepper, ¼ cup diced canned pimiento, and ⅓ cup stuffed green olives, sliced. Pour into 8½x4½x2½-inch loaf pan. Chill till firm. Garnish with carrot curls and ripe olives.

GERMAN PERFECTION MOLD

Pour two 3-ounce packages mixed vegetable-flavored salad gelatin into an 8½x4½x 2½-inch loaf pan. Add 2 cups boiling water; stir to dissolve gelatin. Add 1 tablespoon vinegar and 12 to 15 ice cubes; stir constantly till gelatin begins to thicken (about 3 minutes); remove any unmelted ice.

Snip into the partially set gelatin the tops of 6 or 7 small green onions, and 1 canned pimiento. Cut through the contents of one 1-pound can (2 cups) sauerkraut; add to gelatin; stir gently. Chill till firm. Unmold on greens. Serves 8 to 10.

Here's a slick trick for mincing parsley. Rinse parsley thoroughly. Cut off stems; put the tops in measuring cup. Hold kitchen scissors with points down in cup of parsley. Snip-snip till leaves are finely cut.

Gay garnish: *Onion Mums.* For each, peel a large white onion. *Cutting only to ½ inch from bottom,* slice down center; cut in quarters; cut quarters in eighths. Add food coloring to warm water in bowl (enough to cover onion). Add onion; let stand till colored.

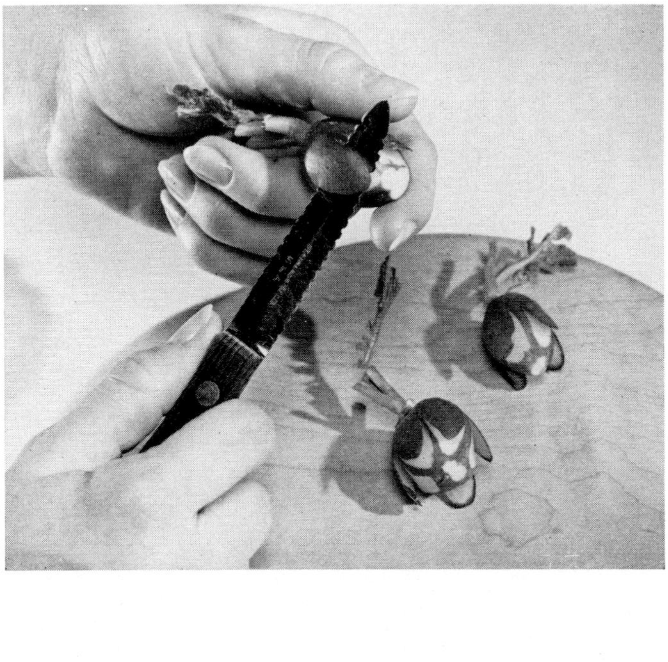

Radish Roses (at left) pretty up a salad or relish tray.

Cut off root of radish, then cut four or five thin petals around radish, leaving bit of red between. Use grapefruit knife or tip of paring knife. Chill in ice water. If desired, heap on crushed ice to serve.

Radish Accordions: Select long red radishes. Cut not quite through in 10 to 12 narrow slices. Chill in ice water so slices will fan out.

Radish Dominoes: Cut radish at root end to make a deep X. Now slice off thin circle of red peel in center of each quarter. Leave on tops. Chill.

Fluted Mushrooms skewered with cherry tomatoes make a high-style trim!

Wash and remove stems from large, well-shaped mushrooms. Using a sharp, short-bladed knife, start from center top of mushroom and cut about ¼ inch deep in curving line to bottom. Starting from same point, slant the knife slightly, and make a second cut parallel to first and ¼ inch apart. (This frees mushroom strip between cuts.) Leaving ¼-inch space, flute again. Repeat around mushroom.

Pour boiling water over; drain. Brush with lemon juice. String on skewers, top side up, with tomatoes.

Carrot sticks get a dressed-up look! For a change, cut sticks with a waffle cutter.

To make *Carrot Curls,* first pare carrots. Then cut thin lengthwise strips with vegetable parer. Rest carrot on board; pare away from you. Roll up long slices, toothpick to hold. Chill at least 1 hour in ice water. Remove picks before serving.

Short on time? Make *Carrot Crisps:* With parer, slice carrot crosswise; chill thin circles in ice water—they ruffle prettily.

More crunchy relishes—*Celery Fans:* Cut celery stalks in 3- or 4-inch lengths. Make parallel cuts close together from one end almost to the other. Or slit both ends almost to center. Chill in ice water till strips curl.

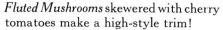

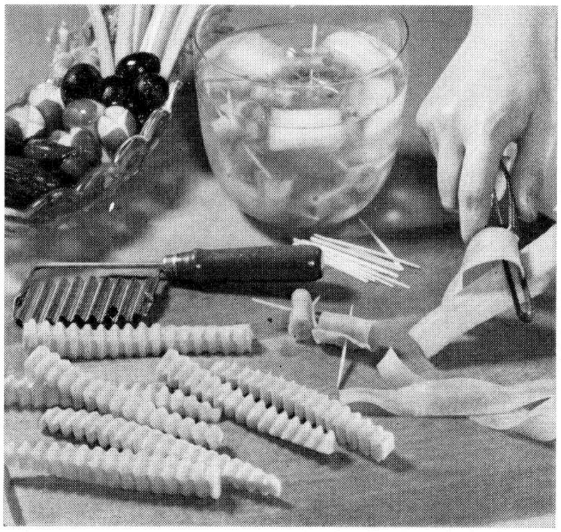

With these two handy gadgets in your collection, making egg slices or wedges is a snap—and the results look so professional! In fact, once you use these tools, you'll wonder how you ever kept house without them.

Egg wedger, at left, works like a pair of scissors to turn out six pretty hard-cooked egg wedges—just right to top a bowl of potato salad or toss into chef's salad bowl. If you like, arrange wedges to make "sunflower." For petals, place wedges, cut side down, in a circle atop salad; mound of sieved egg yolk makes sunny golden center. Pimiento strips add finishing touch.

Egg slicer, at right, separates an egg into eight perfect slices—makes a quick trim for creamed vegetable.

canning and freezing

Peter Piper picked a peck of pickled peppers . . . where's the peck of pickled peppers Peter Piper picked? No one will ever determine just how Peter managed to pickle a pepper before it was picked. Nevertheless, this childhood tongue twister symbolizes man's age-old concern for preserving his precious food supply.

Primitive methods of food preservation are recorded throughout history. Man discovered fire. Sometime later, he probably accidentally dropped meat into the flame—a rude beginning to prevent spoilage. Ancient inhabitants of a cold climate may have been snowed-in while trying to retrieve their game; only to find the animal meat still in good condition at the following spring thaw. Our frugal ancestors learned that salt, smoke, vinegar, and sugar would help keep their scrawny harvest through the long, lean winter months ahead.

Modern research is still striding forward, perfecting new and better ways to preserve our home-grown food. The up-to-date methods presented in this chapter rest upon years of scientific research, in order to bring you the easiest and safest canning and freezing procedures to capture the bounty of your summer garden.

DEFINITION OF TERMS

Acid food—Tomatoes, ripe pimiento peppers, sauerkraut and some pickled products.
Low-acid food—In this group are all vegetables except those noted above.
Enzymes—Natural substances found in all vegetables. If not destroyed by cooking they cause changes in color, texture, and flavor of canned and frozen food.
Blanching—Boiling food for a few minutes, then dipping in cold water. This retards the activity of enzymes when vegetables are prepared for freezing.
Bacteria, molds, and yeasts—Low forms of plant life known as microorganisms. These organisms exist everywhere. When not destroyed by cooking they grow in canned food and cause it to spoil.
Spoilage—Canned foods are spoiled when they "work," mold, have unnatural odor, become "cheesy," sour, or otherwise unfit to eat. Spoiled food should be destroyed.
Processing—Cooking jars of food in a steam pressure canner (low-acid foods) or boiling water bath (acid foods) long enough to destroy bacteria, enzymes, molds, and yeasts.
Pack—Manner in which food is put into jar.
Cold or raw pack—To fill jars with raw food to be processed.
Hot pack—To fill jars with hot food, either precooked or cooked, to be processed.
Precooking—Boiling, steaming, or baking vegetables for a few minutes, then using the hot pack method for canning.
Headspace—The amount of space left at the top of the jar after packing it with food and liquid. (Proper headspace is important in retaining liquid in the jar.) This term also refers to the amount of space left at the top of a freezing container to allow for expansion of the food during the freezing process.
Partly seal—To leave caps or lids loose while jars are being processed. All jars on which regular jar rubbers are used must be partly sealed while in canner, and closed airtight as soon as removed from canner. This does not apply to the two-piece metal cap which is self-venting during processing.
Vacuum seal—When applied to sealing, vacuum refers to the absence of normal atmospheric pressure in jars; sealing means closing the jars airtight.
Venting or exhausting—Forcing air to escape from a jar or permitting air to escape from a steam pressure canner.

ASSEMBLING EQUIPMENT

For good results, you'll need canning equipment that is in tiptop shape!

Jars and lids must be flawless—no nicks, chips, or cracks. If a jar doesn't measure up, discard it. Get all new self-sealing lids or rubbers. If bail on glass-top jar is loose, remove bail; bend down in center; bend in sides to snap back in place.

Wash jars and lids, except those with sealing compounds, in sudsy water; rinse. Some metal lids with sealing compounds need boiling; others only a dip in hot water; follow manufacturer's directions.

Steam-pressure canner. To clean the petcock and safety-valve openings, draw a string or pipe cleaner through.

Check pressure gauge so you'll know you're getting the right processing temperatures.

A weighted gauge needs thorough cleaning. A dial gauge, whether it's old or new, must be checked before the canning season and during the season if your canner gets frequent use. You can ask your dealer, manufacturer, or country home demonstration agent where to have it checked.

Thoroughly clean canner kettle. But keep the cover out of water; wipe it with a sudsy cloth, then a damp cloth. Dry.

Water-bath canner. You can use any big metal container with a cover that's deep enough to have an inch or two of water over tops of jars and a little extra space for boiling. You'll need a rack to keep jars from touching the bottom.

GLASS JAR CLOSURES

A flat metal lid with sealing compound and metal screw band fits the standard Mason jar. When the band is screwed firmly, the lid has enough give to let air escape during processing. This lid is self-sealing—do not tighten further after processing.

Several kinds of two-piece metal caps are available. Follow manufacturer's directions for using metal caps.

In some areas you may find the porcelain-lined zinc screw cap with rubber ring that fits standard Mason jars. In others, the wire-bail type of glass jar with glass lid and rubber ring is available. For tapered shoulderless jars, use flat metal lids and screw bands.

Following the jar closure directions carefully will insure a satisfactory seal.

GENERAL CANNING PROCEDURES

Select high quality—The initial produce determines the quality of the canned product. Choose only fresh, young, tender vegetables. Time is of the essence—can them quickly before they lose their freshness! If you garden, "2 hours from garden to can" is a good rule of thumb. Vegetables from nearby garden stands are next best to your own home-grown products.

Use only the perfect produce. Prepare just enough vegetables for one canner load at a time. Sort each vegetable according to size and ripeness to insure even cooking. Store vegetables in a cool, airy place if they must be held before canning.

Wash thoroughly—Wash all vegetables thoroughly regardless of whether they will be pared. Dirt contains some of the bacteria hardest to kill. Wash small lots at a time, under cold, running water or through several changes of water.

Lift the food out of the water each time so dirt that has been washed off won't go back on the food. Rinse pan thoroughly between washings. Don't let vegetables soak; this causes loss of flavor and food value. Handle gently to avoid bruising.

YIELD OF CANNED VEGETABLES FROM FRESH

The number of quarts of canned food obtained from a given amount of fresh vegetables depends on quality, condition, maturity, and variety of the vegetable, size of pieces, and on the way the vegetable is packed—raw or hot pack.

For 1 quart of canned food, it takes the following amount of fresh vegetables, as purchased or picked:

	Pounds
Asparagus	2½ to 4½
Beans, Lima in pods	3 to 5
Beans, snap green	1½ to 2½
Beets, without tops	2 to 3½
Carrots, without tops	2 to 3
Corn, sweet, in husks	3 to 6
Peas, green, in pods	3 to 6
Squash, winter	1½ to 3
Sweet potatoes	2 to 3
Tomatoes	2½ to 3½

PACKING METHODS

Most vegetables may be canned two ways: cold pack (raw) or hot pack (precooked). Which method produces the better flavor and texture is a matter of personal preference. The detailed instructions must be followed precisely—there are no short cuts!

1. Wash jars and caps; rinse. Place in hot water till you are ready to fill jars. You don't have to sterilize the jars—the processing takes care of that. If canning acid food, place water bath canner on heat with enough water to cover jars over top.

2. Wash and trim vegetables according to the chart on page 156.

3. Pack the vegetables into the jars using either the cold or hot pack method.

Cold Pack. Asparagus, Lima and green beans, carrots, corn, peas, and tomatoes may be packed by this method. Pack vegetables firmly into jars, (except corn, Limas, and peas; pack loosely). Leave ½-inch headspace at top of jar; (1-inch for corn, Limas, and peas). Pour boiling water into jars leaving ½ inch headspace for all vegetables (except peas; leave 1½ inches).

Hot Pack. All vegetables may be packed by this method. Precook for the time indicated on the chart (page 156). Pack boiling hot vegetables loosely into jars, leaving a ½-inch headspace. (Leave a 1-inch headspace for corn, Limas, and peas.) Pour cooking liquid or boiling water into jars still leaving the same headspace.

4. Chase out air bubbles from filled jars by working blade of knife down sides of jars. This helps keep liquid above food—food at top won't darken. Add more liquid if needed, but keep headspace.

5. Add 1 teaspoon of salt to each quart.

6. Wipe sealing edge of jars with clean cloth to remove food particles. Adjust jar caps. For self-sealing caps, put flat metal lid on jar with composition next to glass and screw the band tight. Partially seal jars with rubber rings and zinc caps by screwing caps down firmly, then turning caps back ¼ inch. For glass-top jars, click the longer wire over top of lid and leave the shorter wire up.

7. Process immediately in a pressure canner (see processing, page 152), using times indicated on the chart (page 156). *Only tomatoes and sauerkraut may be safely processed in a water bath* (see processing, page 152). Note high altitude changes, page 151.

CANNING TIPS

- Pack starchy vegetables—corn, peas, Limas—loosely with plenty of hot water. Fill only to within 1 inch of top to allow for expansion during processing and thorough cooking.
- Do not fill jars too full or liquid will be forced out during processing.
- One tablespoon vinegar to each quart of beets will help retain color.
- Cooking liquid is recommended for packing most vegetables because it may contain minerals and vitamins dissolved out of the food. Boiling water should be subtituted if the cooking liquid is dark or strong-flavored, or if there is not enough liquid.

Check manufacturer's instructions for filling and sealing jars. Set out all equipment and utensils needed. Check jars. Be sure there are no nicks, cracks, or sharp edges. Use new lids.

Stand hot jars on wood or cloth. Pack washed, drained beans loosely into jars; cover with boiling water leaving ½-inch headspace. Add 1 teaspoon salt to each quart of beans.

Wipe top and threads of jar with clean, damp cloth to remove all food particles. A speck of food will break the seal. Put lid on, sealing compound next to jar. Screw band down evenly.

HIGH ALTITUDE

Processing times given apply to a specific food prepared according to directions at sea level. Correct this cooking time or pressure to match the altitude at different locations.

For a pressure canner, increase the 10 pounds of pressure 1 pound for each 2,000 feet above sea level.

For water bath, add 1 minute to the processing time, if time specified is 20 minutes or less, for each 1,000 feet above sea level. Add 2 minutes for every 1,000 feet if the time called for is more than 20 minutes.

PROCESSING

Pressure canner. Place jars on rack in canner containing 2 to 3 inches boiling water. Leave space between jars so steam can circulate freely. Fasten canner cover securely. Exhaust all air by letting a steady flow of steam escape for 10 minutes before closing the petcock.

Start counting processing time when gauge reaches specified pressure. Keep pressure constant by adjusting heat. Do not lower pressure by opening petcock. When processing time is up, remove canner from heat and *let pressure drop to zero.* Then open petcock slowly and unfasten cover.

Adjust the caps on jars. Place jars in wire rack and insert filled rack in steam-pressure canner containing the amount of hot water recommended by the manufacturer.

Place canner over heat and adjust cover according to manufacturer's instructions. Leave vent open till steam escapes steadily. Process jars according to chart on page 156.

Stand jars several inches apart out of drafts to cool. Test seal by pressing center of lid. If dome is down or stays down when pressed, the jar is sealed. Store jars in a cool, dry, dark place.

Pressure pan. Pints may be processed in a pressure pan providing the pan has an accurate gauge for controlling pressure and can be operated at 10 pounds. Allow 20 minutes longer than the time required to process the food in a pressure canner.

Water-bath. This method is only safe for processing tomatoes or sauerkraut. For cold pack have water in canner hot but not boiling; for hot pack have water boiling. Lower jars into canner slowly; be sure jars do not touch. Cover. Count time when water comes to rolling boil. Keep water boiling gently during entire time. Add more *boiling* water during processing if needed to keep containers covered.

AFTER PROCESSING

Sealing and cooling. Do not tighten self-sealing caps after processing. Seal jars with jar rubbers and zinc caps immediately after processing by screwing lid down tight. Seal glass-top jars by lowering the shorter wire. If liquid boiled out during processing, *do not open jar* to add more. Seal the jar just as it is.

Cool jars upright on a thick cloth or rack, never on a cold surface. Avoid drafts. Leave space between jars so air can get to all sides for even cooling.

Testing seal. Check the seal on jars when the jars are cold. To test a jar with a flat metal lid, press center of lid; if lid is drawn down, jar is sealed. When other types of caps are sealed, jars won't leak when you tip them.

If a jar isn't sealed, you can use the food immediately; or check jar, and reprocess food at once with a new lid.

Storing jars. Carefully remove the screw bands from the self-sealing flat metal lids. Stubborn bands may be loosened by covering with a damp hot towel for a moment. Wipe containers clean. Label jars to show contents, date of canning, and lot number if you canned several lots that day.

Store jars in a cool, dry, dark place. Dampness may corrode metal lids and cause leakage. Warmth affects the quality of canned food. Freezing may crack a jar or break the seal causing spoilage.

Opening jars. When you open jars with rubbers, pull the rubber out with pliers. To open self-sealing jars, puncture lid and lift up. It's a good idea to use food within a year for best eating quality.

SPOILAGE

Make it a habit to examine canned goods before and after opening them. Keep these spoilage signs in mind: leaks, bulging lids or rings, mold, bubbling, spurting liquid, or off-odor. Never use canned food that shows any of these spoilage signs.

Since some spoilage cannot be detected, *take this precaution with all home canned vegetables: Cook covered in boiling water for at least 10 minutes.* If the vegetable looks spoiled, foams, or has an off-odor during heating, destroy it immediately without tasting.

FREEZING VEGETABLES

Select the best. You cannot have better frozen vegetables than the fresh ones you start with. Choose garden-fresh, slightly immature vegetables. Salad vegetables (lettuce, cucumbers, radishes, cabbage, onion, and celery) lose crispness when frozen, so are not desirable for freezing.

Pick varieties wisely. Some freeze better than others. For information about local varieties, write your state extension service or state agricultural college.

Handle quickly. Freshness wastes away rapidly at room temperature. If you can't freeze vegetables immediately, store in the refrigerator. Freeze as soon as possible.

Prepare carefully. Wash, trim, and sort vegetables according to chart, page 157. Blanching is a must to prevent off-flavors and discoloration, see page 154.

Package properly. This is extremely important. Moisture-vaporproof containers are needed to save flavor, texture, color, and vitamins. Good packaging keeps foods from drying out (freezer burn) and makes the best use of freezer space.

Suitable rigid containers could be: glass, aluminum, plastic, heavily waxed cardboard, or tin. Bags and sheets made of moisture-vaporproof materials such as, heavy foil, cellophane, plastic, or rubber latex are also suitable for wrapping.

Label accurately. Label packages plainly with materials which are moisture-resistant. Include the name of the vegetable and the date it was packed.

Seal. Leave headspace—room for food to expand as it freezes. Follow to the letter the manufacturer's directions for sealing.

Freeze rapidly at 0° or below. The faster the freezing, the smaller the ice crystals formed. So, it's good to freeze small batches. Large lots or large packages freeze much more slowly. For quickest freezing, place packages against freezer plates or coils. Leave a little space between packages for air circulation.

Store at 0° or below. Stored at this temperature, vegetables lose little flavor, color, texture, or nutritive value. Most vegetables will maintain high quality for 8 to 12 months. Keep food frozen until ready for use. Vegetables are low acid foods which spoil rapidly after thawing. If vegetables have thawed, store in the refrigerator and cook as soon as possible. *Never attempt to refreeze vegetables.*

To water blanch vegetables, lower 1 pound of vegetables into 4 quarts of boiling water. Keep heat high. Cover and start timing. Heat cut green beans for 3 minutes.

When time is up, plunge vegetables (here they're peas) into icy water. Chill the vegetables for the same length of time as you heat them. Remove basket from water and drain very well.

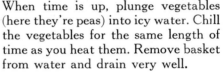

Into the bag goes a scoop of peas. Here the funnel fits on a metal frame that holds the bag open. The rack keeps the cartons erect, pan catches spills. Heat-sealer closes the bag airtight.

BLANCHING VEGETABLES

Blanch vegetables before freezing to stop enzyme action. It helps retain the fresh-picked flavor and appearance. Water blanching is best for most vegetables. Broccoli, sweet potatoes, and winter squash may be blanched using the steam or water method.

Water blanching: Use about 1 pound fresh vegetables. You'll need a large kettle with a lid and a wire-mesh basket, or a blancher. Use at least 1 gallon *rapidly boiling* water. Immerse basket of vegetables and cover.

Start counting the recommended time (see chart)—use a clock with a second hand or a timer. Allow 1 minute longer boiling time at 5,000 or more feet above sea level.

Remove promptly when time is up. Chill quickly by putting basket of vegetables into a pan of *cold* or *ice* water. Change water frequently. Allow about as much time for cooling as for blanching. Drain well.

Pack into containers, allowing ½-inch head space. Seal, label, and freeze.

Steam blanching: Use kettle with *tight-fitting* lid and a low rack to keep vegetables above the water. Add water 1 or 2 inches deep; bring to a *rapid boil.* Maintain enough heat to create plenty of steam throughout the blanching period. Place vegetables in basket on rack. Cover kettle tightly.

Start timing at once—be accurate. Steam 1 minute longer at 5,000 feet or more above sea level. Remove vegetables immediately when time is up. Cool quickly in ice water, as for water blanching.

Pack in containers, allowing ½-inch head space. Seal, label, and freeze.

Make your selection of freezing materials from a wide assortment. Among those most frequently used are heavily-waxed cardboard boxes and cartons, plastic containers, and plastic bags. Remember clear plastic and foil wraps for items like corn on the cob.

Two types of plastic bags are pictured. The lightweight plastic can be sealed with a paper-covered wire strip. The heavier plastic bags can be sealed with a special heat sealing unit. The food frozen in the heavy bags can be heated in the bag in a pan of boiling water.

YIELD OF FROZEN FOOD

The following amounts of fresh vegetables, as purchased, make 1 pint frozen food.

	Pounds
Asparagus	1 to 1½
Beans, Limas in pods	2 to 2½
Beans, snap green	⅔ to 1
Beets, without tops	1¼ to 1½
Broccoli	1
Brussels sprouts	1
Carrots, without tops	1¼ to 1½
Cauliflower	1⅓
Corn, sweet in husks	2 to 2½
Peas	2 to 2½
Summer Squash	1 to 1¼

COOK FROZEN VEGETABLES

Top of range. Boil ½ cup salted water for each pint. Add vegetables in a frozen block (partially thaw corn on the cob and spinach). Cover; separate pieces with fork, if necessary. When water returns to boiling, reduce heat and begin timing (see chart). Cook until just tender.

Oven-cooked. Place frozen vegetable in greased casserole. Top with 1 to 2 tablespoons butter; season. Cover; bake for time given in chart. Stir 15 minutes before cooking time is up and before serving.

Pressure pan. Break apart vegetables. Cook according to pressure pan directions.

BOILING WATER METHOD

Vegetable	Minutes (after return to boil)
Asparagus	5 to 10
Beans, cut green	12 to 18
Beans, French-style green	5 to 10
Beans, baby Lima	6 to 10
Broccoli	5 to 8
Brussels sprouts	4 to 9
Carrots	5 to 10
Cauliflower	5 to 8
Corn, whole kernel	3 to 5
Corn, on the cob	3 to 4
Peas, green	5 to 10
Spinach	4 to 6
Summer Squash	10 to 12

OVEN METHOD

Vegetable	at 325° (minutes)	at 350° (minutes)
Cut asparagus	65	55
Cut green beans	55	45
Baby Lima beans*	50	40
Broccoli	55	45
Whole kernel corn	55	45
Green peas	50	40
Spinach	65	55
Succotash	55	45

*Add 2 tablespoons water before baking.

CANNING GUIDE

Acid vegetable	Preparation	Water bath in min. (Pints)	Water bath in min. (Quarts)
Tomatoes	Scald, then dip in cold water; peel. Cut out stem ends. Pack whole or cut in halves or quarters. Pack in jars; add hot tomato juice. Add 1 teaspoon salt to each quart tomatoes.	35	45
	Tomato Juice: Wash; cut out stem ends; cut up tomatoes. Simmer till soft, stirring. Press through sieve. Add 1 teaspoon salt to each quart juice. Reheat just to boiling. Fill jars to ¼ inch from top.	10	10

Low acid vegetable	Preparation **Precook in boiling water; use hot cooking water to fill jar and pack to ½ inch from top unless otherwise specified; add 1 teaspoon salt to each quart. Or pack raw into jars and cover with boiling water leaving ½ inch headspace; add 1 teaspoon salt to each quart.**	Pressure canner minutes at 10 lbs. (Pints)	Pressure canner minutes at 10 lbs. (Quarts)
Asparagus	*Hot pack:* Wash; bundle; precook in boiling water 3 minutes (tips above water); pack hot. Add salt, hot cooking water.	25	30
	Cold pack: Wash, trim off tough ends. Cut in 1-inch pieces, pack tightly into jars. Add salt. Cover with boiling water.	25	30
Beans **Green and Wax**	*Hot pack:* Wash; break off ends; cut or leave whole; precook 5 minutes in boiling water; pack hot; adding salt and boiling water.	20	25
	Cold pack: Wash and trim beans; cut in 1-inch pieces; pack in jars. Add salt. Cover with boiling water.	20	25
Lima	*Hot pack:* Shell and wash young, tender beans; cover with boiling water and bring to boiling. Pack loosely to 1 inch from the top of jar. Add salt and boiling water.	40	50
	Cold pack: Shell and wash young, tender beans; loosely fill to 1 inch from top of pint jar, 1½ inches from top of quart jar. Add salt. Cover with boiling water leaving ½ inch headspace.	40	50
Beets	Wash, leaving on root and 1 inch of tops. Cover with boiling water; precook about 15 minutes. Slip off skins; pack hot. Add salt, hot water.	30	35
Carrots	*Hot pack:* Wash and scrape; slice or leave small ones whole. Cover with boiling water and bring to boil; pack hot; add salt, hot cooking water.	25	30
	Cold pack: Wash; scrape. Pack tightly into jars; add salt; fill with boiling water.	25	30
Corn **Cream-style**	*Hot pack:* Cut corn from cob, cutting only about half the kernel; scrape cob. Add 1 cup boiling water to each pint of corn; heat to boiling. Pack in hot pint jars, adding ½ teaspoon salt to each pint. Pack loosely and only to 1 inch from top of jar.	85	
Whole kernel	*Hot pack:* Cut corn from cob; do not scrape cob. Add 1 cup boiling water to each pint of corn; heat to boiling. Pack hot to 1 inch from top of jar; pack loosely. Add salt.	55	
Peas	*Hot pack:* Shell; wash. Cover with boiling water; bring to boiling. Pack hot. Pack loosely to 1 inch from top of jar. Add salt, hot water.	40	40
	Cold pack: Shell and wash. Pack loosely to 1 inch from top of jar. Add salt; cover with boiling water leaving 1½ inches headspace.	40	40
Potatoes **New White**	Wash; precook in boiling water 10 minutes; remove skins. Pack hot; add salt; cover with hot cooking water.	30	40
Sweet	*Dry pack:* Wash; precook 25 minutes in boiling water. Remove skins; pack hot to 1 inch from top of jar. Press gently. Add no liquid or salt.	65	95
	Wet pack: Wash; boil till skins slip off easily. Remove skins. Pack hot, leave 1 inch space at top of jar. Add salt. Cover with boiling medium syrup (4 cups water to 3 cups sugar).	55	90
Squash **Winter**	Wash; remove seeds; cut in pieces; pare. Barely cover with water; bring to a boil. Pack hot. Add salt; cover with hot cooking water.	55	90
	Sieved squash: Wash; remove seeds; cut up; pare. Steam about 25 minutes or till tender. Put through sieve. Heat through, stirring. Pack hot. Add no liquid or salt.	65	80

FREEZING GUIDE

Vegetable	Preparation	Blanching Boiling water	Blanching Steam (on rack over boiling water)
Asparagus	Wash. Trim; cut to 6-inch lengths or in 2-inch pieces. Separate according to size	Small Stalks—2 min. Large Stalks—4 min.	
Beans **Green**	Wash; cut off ends. Cut in pieces, or French.	3 min.	
Lima	Wash pods, shell or leave in pods.	Small—2 min. Large—4 min.	
Beets	Wash and sort according to size. Trim tops, leave ½-inch stems. Cook till tender.	Small—30 min. Medium—45 min.	
Broccoli	Wash; cut into medium pieces 5-6 inches long, no thicker than 1½ inches.	3 min.	5 min.
Brussels sprouts	Cut from stem; wash carefully. Remove outer leaves. Sort according to size.	Small—3 min. Large—5 min.	
Carrots	Wash; scrape or pare. Cut into ¼-inch slices or leave whole if small and tender.	Sliced—2 min. Whole—5 min.	
Cauliflower	Wash; cut into 1-inch thick pieces.	3 min.	
Corn on the cob	Husk, remove silk, wash, and sort ears according to size.	Small—7 min. Medium—9 min. Large—11 min.	
Whole kernel	Plunge ears in boiling water for 4 minutes. Cut off corn.	4 min.	
Greens	Wash thoroughly. Cut and discard thick stems and imperfect leaves. Blanch beet, chard, kale, mustard, and spinach. Blanch collards.	2 min. 3 min.	
Parsnips **Rutabagas** **Turnips**	Remove tops. Wash, peel, cut into ½-inch cubes.	2 min.	
Peas	Wash pods; shell. Discard starchy peas.	1½ min.	
Potatoes Sweet	Cook in water till tender with jackets on. Cool; pare and slice. Dip in solution of ½ cup lemon juice to 1 quart water. Or mash; mix 2 tablespoons lemon juice per quart.	Cook 30-40 min.	Cook 45-60 min.
Squash **Summer**	Wash. Cut in ½-inch slices.	3 min.	
Winter	Cut into pieces and remove seeds. Cook till soft; remove pulp; mash. Cool quickly.	Cook 15 min.	Cook about 20 min.

index

A-B

C-D-E

F-G-H-I

J-K-L-M

N-O-P

Q-R-S

T-U-V

W-X-Y-Z